# Thoughtful Times

# *Thoughtful Times*

## for speaking harsh truths with kindness

Mary Lax

AuthorHouse™
1663 Liberty Drive
Bloomington, IN 47403
www.authorhouse.com
Phone: 1-800-839-8640

© 2014 Mary Lax. All rights reserved.

No part of this book may be reproduced, stored in a retrieval system, or transmitted by any means without the written permission of the author.

Published by AuthorHouse  07/07/2014

ISBN: 978-1-4969-1911-3 (sc)
ISBN: 978-1-4969-1910-6 (e)

Any people depicted in stock imagery provided by Thinkstock are models, and such images are being used for illustrative purposes only. Certain stock imagery © Thinkstock.

Because of the dynamic nature of the Internet, any web addresses or links contained in this book may have changed since publication and may no longer be valid. The views expressed in this work are solely those of the author and do not necessarily reflect the views of the publisher, and the publisher hereby disclaims any responsibility for them.

# Contents

Preface ............................................................................................ ix
Introduction .................................................................................... xv

Chapter 1    Holding On to Faith and Courage............................. 1
Chapter 2    The Role of Truthfulness and Kindness in
                 Handling Fear and Love ............................................ 3
Chapter 3    The Last Chapter ........................................................ 6
Chapter 4    Phoebes ...................................................................... 11
Chapter 5    In the Beginning of Mistreatments Suffered............ 14
Chapter 6    Key References............................................................ 17
Chapter 7    A Child's Lesson on Taking Care of Fear .................20
Chapter 8    A Cat's Lesson on Taking Care of Love .................... 22
Chapter 9    A Beautiful Place—Its Dreams and Its Nightmares.... 26
Chapter 10  How Hurtful Battles Erupt ....................................... 32
Chapter 11  World War II.............................................................. 33
Chapter 12  War Cannot Make Peace ........................................... 35
Chapter 13  Time Out..................................................................... 37
Chapter 14  The Renter.................................................................. 38
Chapter 15  Accidental Cruelty ..................................................... 41
Chapter 16  Grandpa...................................................................... 43
Chapter 17  Harsh Truths We All Must Own .............................. 46
Chapter 18  A Bit More Personal History.................................... 47
Chapter 19  Further Thoughts on Differences............................. 50
Chapter 20  Widowhood ................................................................ 52
Chapter 21  Further Insights in Regard to Close Personal
                  Relationships............................................................... 54

| | | |
|---|---|---|
| Chapter 22 | A Wonderful Friendship | 58 |
| Chapter 23 | Life Is Good | 64 |
| Chapter 24 | Another Fisherman Friend | 66 |
| Chapter 25 | Summer People | 69 |
| Chapter 26 | The Fire Chief and the Fortune Teller | 71 |
| Chapter 27 | My Mom | 73 |
| Chapter 28 | Insistent Calls from Behind | 75 |
| Chapter 29 | The End of My World | 77 |
| Chapter 30 | Life after Death | 79 |
| Chapter 31 | Re-Birthing | 82 |
| Chapter 32 | Circles, Triangles, Squares | 86 |
| Chapter 33 | Secondary Damages | 89 |
| Chapter 34 | Taurus | 91 |
| Chapter 35 | Ducks Unlimited | 93 |
| Chapter 36 | Chloe | 95 |
| Chapter 37 | Abuse of Power and Privilege | 97 |
| Chapter 38 | Recovery | 103 |
| Chapter 39 | The Price of Integrity | 106 |
| Chapter 40 | The River Boat Trip | 108 |
| Chapter 41 | Helping Children Who Suffer Unthinkable Abuse | 110 |
| Chapter 42 | Social-Services Mistakes | 114 |
| Chapter 43 | Health-Care Mistreatments | 116 |
| Chapter 44 | Health-Care Angels | 119 |
| Chapter 45 | Reflections | 122 |
| Chapter 46 | Assuring Truth in Sharing | 125 |
| Chapter 47 | An Artist Friend | 128 |
| Chapter 48 | Growth in Progress | 131 |
| Chapter 49 | Aunt Esther | 133 |
| Chapter 50 | Betrayal | 136 |
| Chapter 51 | Second Thoughts | 138 |
| Chapter 52 | The Generator Project | 140 |
| Chapter 53 | Idle Thoughts | 142 |
| Chapter 54 | Worse Than Unbearable | 144 |

| | | |
|---|---|---|
| Chapter 55 | Fear Handled Fairly Well | 146 |
| Chapter 56 | Closing Comments | 149 |

Postscript ............................................................................................ 153
About the Author ............................................................................... 157
About the Book .................................................................................. 159

# *Preface*

Writing this book has allowed me to more fully accept, without resentment, the most difficult (and possibly the most essential) life lesson:

> There are too many scars—
> whenever evil forces pass by too close
> you pick the scabs
> and then you bleed.
>
> You want to mend life's broken pieces—
> but the edges are too sharp and cut too deep.
> Don't blame yourself.
> You can't fix what you didn't cause.
>
> You've healed yourself too many times—
> you know all there is to know about evil forces.
> They're real—and powerful.
> Don't doubt yourself.
>
> Too often, all we can do about violence and its demons
> is keep safe distance.

Then came a larger, even more profound understanding that seems to best explain the need to write this book. My ease and success with helping "mentally ill" persons develop or regain self-respect and self-trust—essential to effective management of life affairs—isn't primarily attributable to professional training and licenses, or to any other great talent or accomplishment. I simply understand the cause of their suffering and failures. I have to contend with the same handicaps.

We have in common a profound intolerance of dishonesty and cruelty— whether we're the victim, the witness, or the villain. We simply can't oblige requirements that we get along well with persons who are in any way dishonest or cruel.

I also understand that this intolerance isn't the sickness in our world. The real sickness is all the dishonest and cruel ways that an ever-growing number of "mentally healthy" (and mentally ill) folks resort to in desperate attempt to take care of neglected human needs and responsibilities.

Unlike most of my clients, assigned all sorts of sickness labels and mistreatments, I've not had to endure the absolute worst punishments for my failure to oblige unreasonable social requirements. I attribute this difference to my growing up in a family and neighborhood uncommonly adept at taking care of ourselves and each other. So I was spared damages of developmental neglects and misuses. My adult life commitments have taken a more high-risk course, however.

Writing this book has also allowed me to admit a long-carried deep hope that otherwise I doubt I'd have had the courage to claim. That hope is that I might find a way to reach out to those who have become practitioners or victims of dishonest and cruel survival tactics, and to share with them what I know to be far better and more reliable means of self-protection, achievement, and satisfaction. There are moments, even, when I dare hope this book might turn out to be that way.

A question writers are usually asked to address is, "Who is your target audience?" My truthful answer is "everyone." This book addresses a host of all too common dysfunctional, often even destructive, human assumptions and habits; and it offers simple foolproof rules for making needed improvements. A few advance comments, related to this larger view of unhealthy human inclinations, may be the best way to connect with readers who are most apt to find this book worth their investment.

Despite assurances that we should follow our dreams, at least some of us seem to have entered this world with a prewritten script. No matter the path or goal we pursue, invariably, one thing or another that we have absolutely no control over interrupts our intentions.

I wasn't yet school age when I encountered my first harsh lesson on what happens whenever we don't oblige (unreasonable) expectations—when our best efforts don't quite fit parameters of established norms. I recall my father becoming very angry with me when I refused to play with a neighbor child. I understood his intention was to teach me that rudeness isn't acceptable behavior. But he failed to take into account that it was also unacceptable for this playmate to torment me with hurtful untrue remarks. My mother expressed her frustration with a noncompliant daughter by way of angry prayers to God. Both parents pushed me into studies and life choices they thought were better than my deep-seated preferences.

My parents were trying to prepare me for "the real world." For quite a while, this training did help me fit in, in fact—until my husband and I were both stricken with terrible illnesses. Then I had to contend with neglects and abuses those with uncommon health problems run into. We're sometimes even blamed for the lack of available assistance. Nor is there much real help made available to young families suffering unusual loss and hardship. So I concluded that self-reliance was my best option. But this uncommon attitude proved to be unacceptable also, as we who must develop unusual self-reliant attitudes are then misjudged to be socially defiant.

By now I understand how remarkable human differences are assumed to jeopardize an established social order that gives preference to likenesses. Remarkable differences are even at times assumed to be threatening interpersonally. So those of us who must resort to odd ways of taking care of our needs and responsibilities must also contend with all-out efforts to set us straight, or shut us up, or shun or get rid of us.

I pray that this book will help correct such wrong conclusions and thereby help stop resulting neglects and abuses. My claims of expertise in offering this help are founded mostly on my own successful recovery from devastating experiences, and my success in assisting others in their recovery from tragedies and mistreatments suffered.

I've also enjoyed some very appreciative responses to my odd ways, which experiences I think also support my recommendations for correcting mistaken assumptions. A well-known psychologist and author used to drop by the lakeside village restaurant, where I tended bar and played piano, because he liked my music. He thought I must have studied at Julliard and ought to be playing onstage. I explained, "There are more important things I have to do—like parent eight children and help fix a very troubled world." Then he dropped by to talk with me about how I managed to do all that.

I took classes with a philosophy professor from India who welcomed my bold intellectual adventures. I shared with him that I thought the system of logic he taught could be used to prove anything, true or not true. When he challenged this statement, I replied, "I bet I can even use it to prove I'm God." He promised that if I managed to do that, I'd have an A+ grade for the whole year. I received the A+ grade. And this teacher also admitted that, because of what I showed him, he'd have to make some changes in how he taught this course.

Quite a few folks bought my artwork and liked my poems. I couldn't keep up with a local newspaper's request for feature stories on saving precious natural resources. And school was mostly a place of appreciation and encouragement.

So I think my efforts to help make things right in our relationships and in our world are deserving of serious attention. At least let's open our minds and hearts together to the urgent need for more effective ways to put an end to the craziness of viewing human problems in terms of racial or religious or sexual or gender or political or class or cultural differences, or other special privileges or handicaps or needs and preferences.

We all ought to become more appreciative of each other's differences (and likenesses). This can happen only as the word *we* includes all of humankind and the words *I* and *you* are used merely to represent my and your small yet essential parts of all of *us*. There are no better or worse persons, more or less important or deserving needs or gifts, or causes or plights, or careers or backgrounds, or concerns or goals. And no one of us is qualified to pass judgment on another, except in regard to honest caring treatment of self and others and our world, or lack thereof.

*Then there occurred what I think Oprah would
refer to as "an AHA! Moment:"
It crossed my mind that, in all my 83 plus years of
life on earth, I've not ever met a person,
who talks openly with me about our respective fears
and needs. and our loves and ambitions,
with whom I've not felt safe and important.
So I'm quite sure that such conversations are the key
requirement of getting along well with each other,
interpersonally and internationally.*

# *Introduction*

This book has been in the making for most of my adult life, though recently it's taken on a kind of urgency to be finished and published. Yet I keep rewriting this introduction, hoping to find easier and better words for sharing its core message and mission, wanting to wiggle around or cut through staunch impenetrable resistances to (admittedly uncommon) life insights and advice.

Response to this lifelong project, thus far, leaves me with the impression that the one thing most people agree on is that we must not ever dare even consider the possibility that the masterful ways we avoid and deny the root causes and impact of neglect and abuse are what perpetuates this violence. It seems, as well, that most folks would never dare admit that "hurting back" merely increases the burden of pain and fear.

So, by now, I'm feeling that I must shout that this too heavy and horrible burden belongs to all of us. It makes all of us sick, and this overload and sickness can only get worse until and unless we accept ownership of basic underlying problems and the job of solving them.

The first essential step in this direction is to take a hard up-front look at how we all mishandle powerful fears that are natural inevitable byproducts of our truly precarious situation. We let these fears push and pull us into all sorts of destructive escape efforts and battles that we've been fighting for centuries, without achieving any sort of safe or peaceful coexistence. Yet we somehow convince each other and ourselves that this distancing and these wars are good and necessary, even though it's obvious such defensive attempts perpetuate and aggravate the problem of neglect and abuse of human needs and abilities. It's this misuse of life that turns our fears into demons.

Our demon fears are trying with all their might to get us to use God-given instincts and intelligence to better understand the mechanics of threats to well-being, and ways and means to actually alleviate the risks and dangers. The first challenge is to learn to trust and use well the function of human fear. Only then can we stop the insanity of expecting to make our lives and our world safer and more joyful by avoiding and denying horrific mistakes and damages, and refusing to make essential amends.

I find it alarming, also, that my therapy clients and a few close friends—people who have been assigned all sorts of demeaning labels in an attempt to explain their failure to get along well in a social order where deception and bullying prevail—are the only folks I know who seem to fully grasp the importance of taking better care of ourselves and each other; in relieving the torments of demon fears. Because I've survived an unusual number of horrific losses and mistreatments, only rarely resorting to "hurting back" and without ending up in a back ward of a mental institution, it's commonly assumed I must be tougher than the rest of humanity. The truth is I've simply learned to handle demon fears by figuring out how to make at least some improvements in my use of God-given emotions and intelligence.

This realization brings to mind the time a young man I know well called to announce he needed to talk with me about things that were bothering him. He came to my house, sat down in his favorite rocking chair by the woodstove, and rocked a bit too fast and hard as he addressed head-on a number of life-changing shocking experiences and the terrors they left him with. He made no effort to hold back or hide the soul-rending toll of these terrible shocks. After several hours of this grieving, we hugged big and long, and he left. From that moment, almost fifty years ago, we've enjoyed that rare kind of trust where there is no temptation or cause to keep secret from each other or avoid, deny, or disguise the truth, no matter how disturbing.

Another consideration in rewriting this book introduction so many times is that I'm all too aware how tempting it will be for readers to let the true stories shared throughout distract from the reasons I share them. These stories aren't told to impress anyone with my or others' accomplishments or failures. They just seem to be the best way to give substance and validation to the book's message and promise—that truthfulness and kindness in all interactions are the life rules that ensure getting and staying on the course of ending neglect and abuse. The "beautiful" stories reflect what happens when rules of truthfulness and kindness are applied. The "horrible" stories reflect what happens when these rules aren't honored.

There's another important reason for sharing these stories. I've learned that the worst and most common self–other caretaking mistakes are a result of not sharing with each other the neglect and mistreatment personally suffered or committed, and instead trying to prevent or fix these crimes by way of bigger and better efforts of love. Both fear and love are essential and powerful human functions. But they have very different purposes and requirements. The most important of these differences is best explained, I think, in terms of their order or hierarchy. Until and unless the need to feel safe is well attended, it's impossible to attend well the gifts and responsibilities of love.

*Chapter 1*

# Holding On to Faith and Courage

The purpose of life, I believe, is simply to learn about being alive and living, to share our unique collections of personal experience and knowledge with each other, and to lend assistance in applying this understanding. To assure fulfillment of this purpose, all we need do is follow simple life rules of truthfulness and kindness. (All references to truthfulness and kindness assume it's recognized that it's as important to listen with an open nonjudgmental mind and heart as it is to speak without attempt to misrepresent observations, experiences, or intentions.)

In human affairs, there's so much that pushes and pulls us off the course of always being truthful and kind that no part of this work is safe or easy. No matter how we may choose to overlook or justify such deterrents, they are serious handicaps. Therefore my writing reflects my long-felt need to share what I've come to understand about not giving in to hurtful pressures and temptations that handicap learning and sharing, because it's my observation that such mistakes are the breeding ground and fuel of all violence.

Although this isn't a new concern or mission, the insights that underlie this commitment have recently taken a giant leap, leaving me better equipped to remedy my own mistakes at least. This growth is best defined, I think, with reference to the critique of a gentleman who has been most helpful with various writing struggles that have threatened to throw me off the course of my writing intentions. His final words, "It's your book, not anyone else's, and it doesn't matter what anyone else thinks [about it]," hit me hard and well, shoving me back onto clean firm ground.

It's when we're tempted to try to do the impossible, like trying to placate or change others' objections to our best efforts, that we're most susceptible to hurtful influences—I see that more clearly now. My job as a writer is simply to share what I know to be true and important, as best I can. Attempting to do more or less than this is to assume or assign rights and abilities none of us possesses.

The only forbidden ambitions and actions are those that are dishonest and/or uncaring. Reaffirming this awareness takes me to another critical realization. I've not yet met a person, adult or child, who doesn't have the ability to learn to keep thoughts, feelings, and behaviors true and kind, ordinarily defined as "under control," when basic human needs and abilities are well attended. The exception is when damage from neglect and abuse are so terrible as to be irreparable, or there is other severe traumatic or organic brain damage.

Some of us, of course, need more or less caring and guidance than others. Some of us need to have firm limits set that simply don't allow us to "hurt back" or otherwise mishandle disappointment and mistreatment by refusing responsibilities or misusing gifts and privileges.

*We're all parts of each other and everyone and everything.*

*Chapter 2*

# The Role of Truthfulness and Kindness in Handling Fear and Love

There are likenesses and differences among all humans—our abilities and disabilities, our ambitions and interests, our needs and strengths, our appearances and habits, our status and circumstance. These likenesses and differences must be acknowledged and respected by ourselves and each other. Throughout this book, these responsibilities are referred to as *truthfulness* and *kindness*.

We also have in common basic human functions—physical, intellectual, emotional. It's essential that we learn and teach how to care for and use well these basic functions. This book addresses human emotional functions of fear and love, primarily.

Much of our social conditioning discourages this learning and teaching. Well-being and satisfaction can't be understood in terms of what occurs in prevailing protocols and practices. All of truth isn't found in books of knowledge or religious doctrine or sets of social codes. Truth, and its discovery, is always "in process."

We each accumulate and apply a unique collection and arrangement of vital pieces of life information. These pieces must be shared to find their rightful place with everyone else's pieces of the whole of knowledge. Therein we build understanding. The work of collecting and sharing requires meticulous care to assure the gathering, applying, and reporting of unique observations and experiences are authentic.

Probably the most crippling handicaps of social conditioning are the contradictory demands. We're encouraged to think and act independently, and at the same time we are required to conform to expectations we know don't suit us. Then we have to pretend we're striving to meet unreasonable expectations because it's our choice. Those making harsh judgments and doling out punishments fail to recognize that spontaneity and conformity are opposing orders. Another common double-bind directive is, "You must do this—you will learn to like it," though action by force invariably invites resentment, not appreciative discovery.

A requirement of truthfulness is to talk together (to learn and teach) about things—how they actually are as opposed to how we assume they ought to be. As we talk and listen openly, it's impossible to think of oneself or others as being better or worse than anyone else. This doesn't mean we shouldn't act on whatever we truly believe we have to do along the way of developing understanding. The realization is that the more pieces of truth we gather and share, the better equipped we are to know what is the right thing to do.

Kindness, as referred to in this book, represents acceptance that we are all equally obligated in attending life responsibilities, equally deserving of life privileges, and equally handicapped by all failures in attending responsibilities and by all misuses and denials of life privileges.

Love develops out of understanding, not out of giving way to others' expectations or pursuing strictly self-serving agendas. Fear, in human relationships, is instinctive awareness of threats to well-being—that far too often result from failure to honor requirements of truthfulness and kindness. It doesn't matter who is and isn't "guilty." We're all participants in all mistakes. We all suffer dire consequences. We're all "response-able"—able to respond, to help correct the failure.

Although we can't possibly learn and teach all there is to know in one or many lifetimes, we can come to trust that all (everyone's) pieces of truth are essential, though limited when separated from each other's pieces of truth. Instead of waiting and watching to find fault in each other's views and beliefs, we ought to be seeking ways to make it easier for our own unique pieces of knowledge to find their proper places with others' truths. The temptation we have to guard against, always, is attempting to construct fixed conclusions before we've collected enough reliable information.

> *We must learn to see things through each other's eyes*
> *and what it's like to walk in each other's shoes.*

## Chapter 3

# *The Last Chapter*

This chapter was written after I thought this book was done. I moved it to the beginning as I realized this glimpse of the "here and now" of my life might help readers recognize that I'm actually a rather ordinary kind of person, notwithstanding my odd caretaking rules and habits and compelling heartfelt obligation to help solve huge problems that have plagued humanity since the beginning of life on earth. This story also shows how, at least sometimes, the worst life struggles and the despair they create bring us to a place of having to own and apply neglected dormant abilities just as we're tempted to give in or give up.

It seemed everything in my life was breaking, though I was sure I had done everything necessary to enjoy a safe, snug, productive winter. The plan was to use this time of virtual hibernation to give serious disciplined attention to writing this book, make a few indoor home improvements, catch up with fine-art printing projects, and simply hang out at my great house in the woods. My allergy condition seemed to be fairly well controlled. A close friend made sure I was well stocked with supplies. Health problems weren't quite so troublesome as in the past, despite failures to find needed health-care assistance.

Then, within a couple weeks, my sense of well-being was wiped away. My sewage pump stopped working. Electric power went out for the whole day as the temperature stayed well below zero, and my generator failed to kick in. The pilot light on the porch propane stove stopped working and wouldn't restart. All this happened during the holidays when help with this kind of emergency isn't available in this part of the country.

I hadn't yet recovered from that bunch of troubles when, on the coldest day of winter, my car wouldn't start. After messing around in the bitter cold when a neighbor came to help jump-start it, all the while breathing deadly exhaust, I suffered a bad allergic reaction.

A neighbor who is a first responder was quite concerned about my dangerously high blood pressure. As she asked me about my health history, I admitted to not taking my blood-pressure medicine because of miserable side effects. I felt obliged to also explain my difficult relationships with doctors—how most aren't sympathetic with the handicaps of unusual allergies, especially as allergic type side effects forbid using some medicines that doctors are prone to prescribe for common health problems. I even shared with her the letter I sent to the local hospital and clinic hoping for a helpful response, which I never received. (The hospital director did eventually call me, but only to explain that the hospital and clinic are entirely separate and that she would pass my letter on to the clinic director.) The letter:

To Whom It May Concern,

> This letter is a desperate plea for help with serious health problems. The need is for doctors and other health-care workers to give due account to my extreme sensitivity to various products not commonly recognized as toxic—a number of medications and airborne substances (especially formaldehyde-based, like perfumes), and chemicals in many cleaning and skin-care products.
>
> By now self-protective instincts simply won't let me enter a building that reeks of offensive airborne substances or ingest medication unless there is obvious care to assure due consideration is given to known and suspected intolerances. There is also zero tolerance of insensitive cruel reactions to my efforts to avert serious mistakes.

I realize it's difficult for persons who don't suffer severe allergies to understand the importance of such precautions. I learned long ago to give great care to informing all involved in providing health-care assistance as to my unusual sensitivities, and how there have occurred far too many near fatal mistakes, in hopes that this information will encourage due precautions. But reactions to this effort are more defensive than appreciative, causing me to feel the preference is to not have to put up with me at all. Then, if/when the dreaded errors do occur, the persons responsible become angry with me.

My contention is, still, that I'm entitled to services promised, or at least up-front admission that there's inability or unwillingness to provide me even ordinary health care. It should not be necessary for me to have to beg or shout to have my ordinary and special needs acknowledged, or for me to go to a facility where toxic substances make me rush out of the building gasping for fresh air. And when I present symptoms known to be possible side effects of a prescribed medication, this information should be given due attention. All that I share, in fact, should be accepted as true and important until/unless it becomes known that I'm intentionally lying or incapable of providing true information.

My current pressing health problem relates to blood-pressure medication that I've taken for a number of years, prescribed when I suffered a bad reaction to a prior blood-pressure medicine. This new medicine was selected, I was told, because it's "the safest." Initially, it in fact seemed to be working well. But then came odd allergic symptoms—weird muscle and back pain, eczema like skin eruptions, dizziness, stomach and intestinal upsets with diarrhea (that keep me homebound), insomnia, and frightening bouts of rapid irregular heartbeat. I've of course complained of all these symptoms, with ongoing questioning if they might be side effects of the medicine. Reactions to my questions aggravate my concerns, as they're disregarded with remarks like "not possible."

Well, a couple weeks ago, all these torments became so intolerable I stopped taking this medicine. After just a few days I was able to stoop, bend, and climb stairs without agonizing pain. Skin eruptions are healing. Dizziness is minimal. Gastric pain and diarrhea are gone. I'm sleeping through the night, except when too worried about the lack of respect and caring, and other mistreatment. And I've not had further out-of-control heartbeat bouts.

Then I learned all these symptoms aren't unusual side effects of this medicine. But I also learned I probably shouldn't have stopped taking it "cold turkey." I still need help with blood pressure and other less serious health problems. And my trust is broken.

So now I must simply ask which of your staff doctors, if any, might be so kind as to admit and remedy mistakes and disrespects described?

Sincerely, Mary Lax

Although there was no direct response to my outcry, the caring first responder somehow arranged for me to meet with a doctor in a room in the hospital that was free of offensive airborne substances. This doctor was helpful. I intend to continue to use this help as needed.

I was also struggling with a number of more common aggravations that are constant reminders of the importance of simply refusing all policies, procedures, directives, and misjudgments that disregard human sensitivities, abilities, needs, and limitations. Such aggravations invariably cause me great concern, as I'm reminded how few of us are willing to speak up and speak out, to say, "No! I'll not ignore, support, excuse, cooperate with, or be quiet about untrue, unkind statements or cruel actions against myself or another honest caring person."

As I was back on course with this commitment, I also reclaimed confidence that I was doing all that I could to help make things right in a very troubled world.

The larger understanding that underlies this mission is that all defense attempts that involve action against, away from, or in compliance with offenders and abusers, feed and give power to the evil they represent. The only action that makes good sense is to starve evil—to neither ignore nor deny its prevalence and damages, to refuse to engage in battle with those who resort to heinous crimes, and to not give in to unreasonable hurtful threats and demands. I think this observation alone explains the failures of most current and past efforts to end violence.

*Chapter 4*

# *Phoebes*

When relationships with fellow humans are wrought with pain and disappointment, I'm inclined to seek comfort in remembering good times with great animal friends. Animals rarely resort to unkindness unless tormented, and it seems they're incapable of dishonesty. The following story is about one such friendship.

I was working late, almost ready to leave my therapy offices. It was snowing hard; I wondered if I should cancel the scheduled home visit with a family who lived in the country outside a neighboring town forty miles away. As I was locking up my offices, a lady waiting to clean them insisted that I accompany her to a house a few blocks away "to meet someone special who really needs you." I went with her to meet a sheepdog whose owner was getting married. The wife-to-be was allergic to dogs. (I wondered how the cleaning lady knew I favored sheepdogs.)

This dog, of course, became mine instantly. She went with me to the new clients' home with the understanding that she must follow explicit instructions as to how to behave in the car during this two-hour counseling session. When I returned, she was sitting in the driver's seat, paws on the steering wheel—but, as instructed, she hadn't barked or made a mess or scratched the leather upholstery.

It was quite late when we arrived home. I had to shovel a long driveway by hand with over two feet of accumulated snow. While I shoveled, this dog—already my best buddy—walked the perimeter of the property as though she knew it was her job to assure all was well. She then propped herself against the back door, holding it open for me to haul firewood inside. I had no dog food, so we shared a dinner of leftovers. My possessive male cat put up a fuss but eventually allowed the new family member to sleep close to him next to my bed.

This was the beginning of a long and wonderful relationship. I gave this animal the name Phoebes. Babes, the name she came with, just didn't suit her. From the beginning, she was an active participant in every event and project. She even dug me out of a snow bank when I climbed on top of it on skis to take a photo and its crust gave way, leaving me buried in snow over my head.

Phoebes stayed by my side when I was too sick with pneumonia to take care of her, licking my hot face until the fever broke and the sweat came. She was always excited to be with my son away at school. If I happened to mention he'd be home for the weekend, she'd go to his room to sit by the window until he drove up the driveway. She let a young granddaughter rearrange her long fuzzy eyebrows for hours without complaint.

One hot summer day, when I was weed-whacking my property's roadside ditch, I looked up to find a wolf much too close, growling at me through clenched teeth. Phoebes, inside our fence, ran to my aid, ignoring my command to "Stay!" She jumped the fence and, as I watched in awe, gave plenty of room to the hostile wolf as she deftly maneuvered around me and him to his back side and then gently urged and guided him away from me, along the path between my fence and my neighbor's, through the neighbor's open gate, and into the kennel from which he had escaped. This neighbor raised and trained wolf cubs for movie sets.

He was watching this scene with his gun cocked, expecting he would have to shoot the wolf.

This story made it to the neighboring small town within hours. Phoebes received a hero's welcome whenever we drove into town after this amazing rescue.

## Chapter 5

# *In the Beginning of Mistreatments Suffered*

The requirement to face head-on cruel ugly parts of life on earth first took charge way back in the early 1960's. My wonderful life was crumbling, literally. I was ill—"dying," the doctors said, though no cause could be determined. I was sure I knew the cause all along because I was sure all the bizarre crippling body changes started after massive doses of Novocain for emergency vein-stripping surgery and because of prior bad reactions to local anesthesia. But my observations were dismissed as "impossible" and therefore unworthy of serious consideration.

My husband was ill also. At my insistence, he agreed to have a thorough medical checkup. But doctors agreed with him that his heartbeat irregularities and bouts of chest pain, weakness, and shortness of breath were simply from excessive stress. They didn't consider his father's premature death from coronary artery disease significant.

My husband's mother, who suffered from drug and alcohol addiction, lived with us after her second husband died until, as her behavior became increasingly destructive, I insisted she would have to find her own place to live. My husband, his mother, doctors, family, and friends all resented and fought against my efforts to handle these and other serious problems in an open and direct way. I still believe the outcome wouldn't have been as tragic if I could have found a way to enlist needed assistance and support. It's taken most of the rest of my life to accept that the failures were not mine, that I did everything humanly possible to obtain needed help.

Eventually, I relied entirely on my own good sense in handling my illness. I stopped taking medicines I was sure were causing new and worse symptoms. I adopted a simple diet of unprocessed foods and spent more time outdoors, as I found ways other than excessive clothing to protect open skin lesions from exposure to direct sun. Gradually, those sores healed. Upper arm, shoulder, and neck muscles that had wasted away so that I couldn't even raise my arms above my head grew back, and seizure-like muscle spasms stopped.

My husband's mother died from drug and alcohol overdose. My husband died of massive coronary heart attack. There's more to tell about my health condition and its course, my mother-in-law's and husband's deaths, and related abuses, but here I want to share the events of the day my husband died because they represent the shift in attitude that I'm convinced has to happen to prevent such tragedies in my life, your life, and in the world. Unfortunately, this shift came too little too late for my family.

My husband became more trusting of my unpopular and obstinate ways of caring as he recognized my remarkable recovery had to be the result of my taking charge of my life-threatening illness. Yet I was somewhat surprised when he made an urgent request that I go to court with him on this eventful morning, admitting, "I just need you to be with me."

He was to represent the interests of persons managing a riverfront restoration project. I don't recall the actual issues contested. I do recall how invested my husband was in winning this lawsuit, and how well he developed and presented his arguments. This project was of special interest to him because his father had been a riverboat captain.

I was, of course, bothered by how hard he pushed himself during that court hearing, and I worried about the physical and emotional toll. During one recess, he wept as he hugged me close and cried, "I'm so sorry I've fought against your caring."

When the court hearing was over, we decided to spend the rest of the day just being together. We ran a few errands, had lunch, and talked about everything, especially our love for each other, our great kids, our problems, and our fears. We decided to take the next day off and treat our children to a trip on the riverboat their grandfather had been in charge of building. Our children were allowed to visit the captain's quarters and even take turns at the wheel while we were aboard.

My husband died that night. I was devastated by this worst possible loss, but I'm ever appreciative of that last day with him. If our strong love and trust of each other hadn't been reaffirmed before he died, I'm doubtful I would have survived the cruel punishments for not giving way to unreasonable demands, which are ongoing. I must still put up with all-out attempts to punish the messenger every time I find myself in the difficult position of having to somehow enlist attention to life-threatening circumstance or life-essential interventions that everyone else is bent on ignoring or denying.

It even seems, at times, as if all the torments suffered during and since the tragic loss of my husband have turned into motivation and preparation for writing this book. So now I must contend with an insistent inner taskmaster that won't let me rest each day until I've given my best effort to making known the far-reaching destructive impact of punishing the messenger, how ignorance and denial of harsh truths is the root cause of all violence, what we all must do to honor inherent responsibilities, and how this shift in thought and interaction is the key requirement for correcting human neglects and abuses.

I understand how tempting it is to disregard this effort, how skilled we've all become at justifying the refusal of disturbing messages. I also realize it's everyone's right, and possibly felt need, to dismiss this plea. But then you must concede, in turn, that my felt need to share what I know to be true and important is surely as valid. Please take a few moments to imagine how different this story might be if doctors and other involved persons had taken seriously my pleas for attention to my husband's symptoms of heart disease.

## Chapter 6

# *Key References*

I'm reminded of how my references to truthfulness and kindness, and fear and love, differ from common usage. A little additional effort to explain this difference seems warranted.

I use the words *fear* and *love* to define primary human emotions. As already mentioned, *fear* represents instinctive awareness of threats to well-being; *love* represents instinctive awareness of potentials of life satisfaction (of needs, desires, ambitions, etc.). We must do the work of determining what is the actual threat or potential that's outstanding, its likely impact, and the best protective or pursuant action to employ. Attending this responsibility requires considerable skill and care, abilities that aren't as well taught or applied as we're inclined to assume. We're apt to react however our instincts happen to push us.

Raw fear pushes us to act out in one of two ways: to fight against or to flee from the perceived danger (and/or persons identified as the cause). Raw love pushes us to act out in one of two ways as well: to try to take possession of objects we desire (and/or persons identified as their keepers) or to try to rid ourselves of strong desires and their torments. Instinct alone works on behalf of personal protection and satisfaction whether or not we consciously choose such a course, but not as effectively as is necessary in civilized society.

When fear isn't well attended, it overrides love and all other essential life functions. Other needs and abilities can't be well attended when fear takes control. When fear is well managed, however, we prevent its progression to anger, hate, depression, or other powerful emotional interference with essential functions. Though fear is commonly referred to as negative (or bad) and love is commonly referred to as positive (or good), these are misleading assignments. Both fear and love are integral to our well-being. It's our efforts to ignore, deny, or get rid of their demands for our attention that make them seem troublesome.

Ignoring, denying, or trying to get rid of feelings of fear or love and their functions because of intense emotional discomfort we've not learned to handle well is senseless. It's akin to ignoring, denying, or trying to get rid of one's head or legs and our need of their functions because of intense discomfort we've not yet found right ways to alleviate.

The popular slogan and belief that "the only thing to fear is fear itself" is surely not an outgrowth of understanding emotional functions; it instead seems to be a declaration of an all-out effort to avoid rudimentary inherent human vulnerabilities and related responsibilities.

By now I'm willing to guarantee that if/when we undo the craziness of expecting and trying to circumvent or discard essential human belongings—instead of correcting mistakes in handling them—we will have fixed what is at "the root of all evil." This surely isn't a pompous claim of any sort of special insight or achievement on my part. This plain truth waits, *begs*, to be recognized by anyone willing to take an honest look at his or her own fears. What provokes their taking hold? What do they represent? How does fear turn into anger and rage, eventually erupting in hurtful outbursts, reactions, and internal chaos if not managed responsibly?

Think about the word *danger*; by omitting the letter *d*, *danger* becomes *anger*, which is a natural and predictable progression of fears not well attended. It's my experience that the best way to learn and teach the requirements and benefits of emotional functions, both fear and love, and to respect their powers and potentials when neglected and when well attended, is by sharing our experiences—telling the stories of our different and similar ways and means of feeling the demands of, and acting on, fear and love. It's important, also, to share the impact of failures and successes in handling emotional responsibilities—telling these stories in the spirit of truthfulness and kindness, with a view to needed improvements.

I'm often told that my uncommon study of human problems isn't easy to relate to or appealing. Most folks prefer to follow established trends, even with obvious reasons to admit that the problems we complain about most can't be solved as long as we don't dare think and act outside prevailing (mistaken) assumptions.

> *To better understand mental illness,*
> *watch what (all) people do when they get scared.*

*Chapter 7*

# A Child's Lesson on Taking Care of Fear

She was three years old, accustomed to having her every need and desire given priority attention. The birth of her baby brother was the focus of unusual excitement in the household. Mom and the new baby were still in the hospital because of minor complications of childbirth. Because Dad had way too much to take care of, loving grandparents and neighbors helped with this young girl's care. She was especially anxious after a visit with Mom and her baby brother in the hospital. Everyone else's needs and concerns seemed more important than hers, and she was trying with all her strength to "be good."

This extraordinary commotion may or may not have contributed to the event that pushed its way to the forefront of all else soon after Mom and her new baby brother came home, when this child, who had never had any major illness, suffered a grand mal seizure, severe and prolonged. She didn't have the elevated temperature that's the most common cause of seizures in young children. Needless to say, this shocking traumatic event put all other concerns on hold. Close neighbors took care of the baby as Mom and Dad rushed their daughter to the emergency room.

Hospital emergency-room activity provokes its own set of terrors, especially when young patients are subjected to blood drawing, hooked up to monster machines, and undressed for more thorough prodding and thumping. But this patient got through all this without great resistance or complaint. Then it was time for "the really tough stuff"—the X-rays that required her to lie perfectly still for more than a few minutes on a hard, cold, elevated table, with hookups to electrodes glued among her curls, and possibly being shut inside claustrophobic contraptions.

*Thoughtful Times*

The doctor in charge was unusually caring in preparing this young patient for these frightening procedures. And she was unusually attentive to his every word and gesture. As she gave assurance that she understood what would be done to her and what she would have to do, the doctor said, "Okay, let's do it!"

She replied, "Okay! You do it first!"

The parents explained it's their practice, whenever their daughter is apprehensive about taking on unusually demanding tasks, to offer to demonstrate what they're asking her to do to show that no serious hurt will result.

*Our children are some of our best teachers*
*when we welcome their sharing of what they instinctively understand.*

*Chapter 8*

# A Cat's Lesson on Taking Care of Love

A friend and customer came to my studio to pick up an order of fine-art prints. He brought a friend along. We critiqued and packaged the prints, and then shared impressions of developments in the fine art print business that seem to us to be kind of absurd, which led to remarks as to absurdities in human affairs, generally. Our professional backgrounds have in common extensive work with children who suffered serious neglect and abuse. We talked about ongoing failures to meet the needs of these children. I mentioned how my professional and personal experiences with such failures contributed to the book-writing effort in progress.

*Thoughtful Times*

Somehow the conversation shifted to Bart Kitty, whom I had to have euthanized after our twenty-seven-year life affair. As I admitted that I still couldn't imagine life without this cat, my customer's friend suggested, "You should write that story."

I replied, "I wouldn't begin to know how to do justice to that relationship."

Then both my customer and his friend said, "Maybe that should be the title of your book?"

Following this conversation, I considered using a title something like "Twenty-Seven Years Living with an Ornery Cat." I realized such a title would be more than a bit misleading. Yet I was impressed with the recurring question, "Why not include in this book the story of my and Bart Kitty's odd ways of taking care of ourselves and each other, where the obvious effort on both sides was learning and teaching, and truthfulness and kindness were clearly bottom-line rules?"

At first, he had no name; he was just a kitty in need of a place to stay while his owner, my son's girlfriend, moved to her new apartment. The girlfriend had neglected to mention the "no pets allowed" clause in her new apartment lease. That "temporary" relocation occurred not long after the death of my son's cat, Taurus, another great guy cat that lived a long, unusually eventful life.

So the timing seemed fortunate for Kitty's entry into my life. These two cats, that never met, seemed in some ways kindred souls. Both were adept at assuring their preferences were well attended, when and how they saw fit. Yet they managed to leave those assumed to be in charge feeling fortunate to be of service.

Kitty easily and thoroughly planted himself in the very center of my life. My wool-sock-clad feet became his favorite resting place. He was inclined to situate himself squarely between me and whatever job I was about to do, sprawling out flat, first on his back and next on his front, unmovable until he was thoroughly massaged on both sides.

His coat of white and black spotted fur remained heavy throughout his long life, despite his shedding at least a third of it every week. To keep the spreading of cat fur under control, a vigorous vacuuming (of Kitty as well as the house) became a twice-weekly ritual. And he made sure he got this treatment whenever the vacuum cleaner was rolled out of the closet.

He hated anything cold and loved everything hot. Whenever the woodstove was in operation, he slept under it. On warmer days, he climbed a crudely built ladder left in place for chimney cleaning to find the hottest patch of asphalt roof. He was a great mouser until he decided "enough of that" and thereafter refused to bother another mouse.

The veterinarian said Kitty should have a proper name. I wracked my brain for a title that suited his moods and habits, which brought to mind an ex-Marine friend, Bart, who was once my boss at a restaurant we ran together. After Kitty was given this new name, he took on a few new traits—like when he entered a room and didn't receive immediate loving attention, he growled a complaint "in your face."

He favored all activities and freedoms of our river home, hardly ever strolling farther than a neighbor's pigpen in back and the river's edge in front. He was the first to greet all guests, and all guests readily accommodated his requirement of at least a few minutes of rubdown before being allowed to exchange greetings with anyone else. He invariably chose to stay closest to the person most allergic to cats.

Bart Kitty was elderly when I made the move to town. Because he didn't handle confinement well, I turned an attached garage into an apartment for him and my dog, Shane. This worked great until, one bitter cold winter night, he must have decided Shane's bed was warmer than his, and switched.

Shane didn't fit into Bart Kitty's bed. He apparently decided to remove Bart from the stolen bed by grabbing his head and pulling hard enough to remove a substantial portion of flesh from this cat's skull. Thanks to an exceptionally skilled team of veterinary surgeons, Bart Kitty's scalp was put back together. But they had to stretch the damaged skin so tight to reassemble the ragged pieces that his eyelids would no longer close all the way and his face took on a slant-eyed appearance. Some of the patched pieces retained their fur growth and some were bald. This replacement of torn infected cranial flesh and skin was so rare that Bart Kitty's recovery was monitored by a group of veterinary trauma specialists attending a nearby convention.

With this frightful mishap and appearance alteration, Bart Kitty's habits and personality made another shift. He refused to stay in the garage apartment and yard, so I let him move into the house to take over my best chair and the fireplace hearth. He became insistent that his water bowl must be kept full and fresh and his food bowl mustn't be spoiled with any foods other than Meow Mix. After a few weeks of this pampering, he also decided he should be carried up and down stairs.

My young granddaughter, in love with Bart Kitty since they first met, was delighted that he was at last cooperative with her intentions to take total charge of him when she visited. Two years later, I built a new home in the country. I was worried this move would be difficult for Bart Kitty, but a few days after he moved into the new home, he made a thorough tour of the place on his own. Long steep flights of stairs became quite manageable as he discovered new soft, warm places to explore and nap. My granddaughter, his best friend and caretaker, was pleased as well. She even instructed her parents, "I think, now, we should all move into Bart Kitty's house."

This life-loving wise cat was quite a fine gentleman to the end. I doubt there's another cat that lived so long, so well, with so many devoted people friends. We all miss him terribly. We're ever grateful to have had the pleasure and honor of knowing him. And not one of us, whenever his name is mentioned, can hold back a smile.

*I think this story represents ordinary often-*
*overlooked ways and powers of love,*
*when all fears are handled truthfully and kindly.*

Chapter 9

# A Beautiful Place—Its Dreams and Its Nightmares

This story begins with my offering a rare wilderness property for sale, as I decided it was time to pass on this possession I had built such a special relationship with over a long and most meaningful span of my life.

I had purchased this property even though it had never been my intention to own such a plot of vacant land. It hadn't been used—by humans—for nearly a hundred years. Only nearby landowners were aware of its existence, it was located off a dead-end country road that served primarily

*Thoughtful Times*

as an entryway into thousands of acres of state forest. This road was maintained primarily to enable forest, wildlife, and fire management.

I was driving a visitor from a large city, showing him this pristine country, as he was thinking he might want to have his own place "way up north." I noticed a half-hidden "for sale" sign at the beginning of that overgrown back road and became curious as to where it might lead. There was no drivable road into the property. We walked in, following what seemed to be an abandoned farm path through a large field to an old fallen homestead. In the center of the field, a family of wolves bathed in the intense sunshine, paying us no obvious attention. Beyond the field and fallen homestead, we discovered a river flowing diagonally through the northwest section, with huge old woods on the far side, probably never bothered by people.

As we drove back through the nearest town, we stopped at the local real estate office, again just out of curiosity. We learned the owner of this property was a woman I was acquainted with. I remembered we'd had an enjoyable conversation. A week later I called her, and we had a good visit.

"Town talk" was that she had refused several generous purchase offers. I revisited the property whenever I felt in need of its naked beauty—once after my best pal sheepdog died. I cried my unbearable grief to the spirits I felt all around, and the wolves answered.

The next day, I stopped by the realtor's office and made a low purchase offer I thought I might be able to afford. My offer was accepted without comment. We worked out a standard contract-for-deed deal that suited both our needs and means. Everything that followed honored that adequate document.

I expected a similar mutually appreciative transaction would follow my recent offer to sell this same property. I wasn't at all prepared for the senseless demands, manipulations, and misrepresentations that followed.

The listing process seemed to follow customary procedure, with minor differences in establishing an asking price. The realtor and I, with a close friend and my dog, walked through the property for half a day as I talked openly about my reasons for selling and desire to find a buyer who could better use and take care of the property.

A purchase offer was presented as coming from "a nice couple from Missouri" who intended to move to this far-north town with their two young sons and concrete business. "They love the property," the realtor added. They hoped to make a one-third down payment and pay the balance over ten years by way of contract-for-deed with 6% interest. Though these terms were different from what I had in mind, I ended up agreeing.

I began to regret this decision after the buyer called me at home and we had a rather strange, mostly one-way phone conversation in which he said several times, "I'm sure, as the need to make changes [in the agreement] arises, we can work those out as we go along!"

This statement brought uneasy feelings. I remember responding, "My intention is that we give care to ensuring both our needs and interests are made clear as we make the agreement," which he seemed to accept.

As it seemed we were both satisfied with the standard purchase agreement, we both signed it. The buyer signed both his name and a company name. I didn't give this great attention at the time and even neglected to question it (I'm told) until after we both signed. When I did admit concerns, the realtor explained that the buyer needed to have an address for his company to get permits and licenses. He gave similar reason for the buyer's expressed need to postpone the closing for up to four months to assure permits and licenses would be granted.

None of the described manipulating and rationalizing made sense to me, especially as the company name on the purchase agreement was "Rooster Valley Farms" (a weird name for a concrete company, I thought). In hindsight, I realize that at the first inkling that "something's not right," I should have more vigorously challenged that signature.

I had blocked it out of mind until later, when numerous irregularities raised all sorts of red flags. But I was told there was nothing I could do to correct mistakes, even though there was no actual Rooster Valley Farms company to be found, except with an address the same as the realtor's, which I was at first told was highly suspicious but later that it isn't unusual.

Then even *that* company listing disappeared. Nor could I find a listing for this company anywhere. My son reviewed all company listings in Missouri and reported that there was no such company on record.

*Thoughtful Times*

There was another request—demand, really—for further postponement of the closing, for another month. The reason given was that baby lambs were being born a month ahead of schedule and the buyer couldn't leave home. As the buyer realized I wasn't swayed by his story and assurances, he resorted to abusive threats. I did eventually agree once again to the requested postponement, which was to be another month, after which there was no actual closing date set for another several weeks. Throughout this final delay, the standard requirement of written request and consent was ignored. I didn't make an issue of this irregularity because, at that point, I just needed to be done with this nightmare.

Then came the work of the contract-for-deed agreement. From the beginning, the buyer seemed to assume he was to take charge of this procedure. I was satisfied with the standard form CFD description of buyer/seller privileges and responsibilities, though I felt need to have further clarification of paragraphs defining buyer obligation "to not waste or damage" the property and "to comply with existing laws."

There was no helpful response to my request for clarification, though I pleaded that the lack of regard for my concerns caused deep worries that there might be remarkable differences in our understanding of these two paragraphs—and if such differences did exist, I needed to have corrections made before signing the CFD agreement. Still, no serious attention was given to my request.

So I employed an attorney's help. My attorney gave my needs more specific and somewhat stronger emphasis in his written request to the title company to include this addendum in the CFD document. This effort provoked unfounded accusations and threats similar to attacks that had occurred in prior phone conversations.

I wasn't aware of the exact wording of my attorney's request to "add an additional term under paragraph 20." When I received a hateful letter from the buyer, I was at a loss as to how to respond, as there was neither intent nor action of disregard on my part.

If there had been respectful attention given to my initial request for clarification of the two paragraphs questioned, I would have signed that first contract-for-deed version, which evidently the buyer had no objection to except for my request for clarification. A number of e-mail and phone interactions followed, essentially nonproductive, primarily a progression of the buyer's demands with a few partial concessions, both changing dramatically from day to day, making it impossible to determine what he was upset about or what he wanted.

The outcome of this exchange was the buyer's eventual request to cancel the purchase agreement. I agreed this was my best option at this juncture. I signed and mailed the cancellation request document.

The buyer changed his mind and refused to sign. He had somehow persuaded the title company representative to remove several paragraphs from the standard CFD agreement, including ambiguous paragraphs I was unable to have clarified. This mishandled document was submitted to me with a demand that I "sign or else."

My reply was that I'd not be bullied further into complying with unreasonable demands and threats, nor would I put up with other mistreatment. Within days, I received an announcement that the buyer was suing me for "specific performance of a vacant land purchase agreement"—though I'd clearly agreed to proceed according to PA terms as soon as the paragraphs removed from the CFD agreement were put back into it.

I was scared and sick from all the senseless maneuvering. I clung desperately to ripped apart trust that somewhere in the chain of command governing buying and selling of land there must be someone who says "No!" with me. Surely it was not allowable to push one's way through and around good laws and standard procedures by way of clever deceptive misuse of their intentions and instruments.

The attorney helping me consulted another attorney more familiar with property laws and disputes. Together, they advised that there was no way to prevent the buyer's lawsuit and that I should seek counsel in the county where the court hearing would be held to avoid unnecessary expenses.

I found an attorney in that county with online access, sent an e-mail explaining the situation, and requesting his help. He replied immediately with a few further questions, and then agreed totally with my contention that I was in no way obligated to sign a document substantially altered without my knowledge or consent, after I had reviewed and given approval, before it was eventually presented to me for signing. He recommended that I pass on his opinion to the realtor, along with a request that copies of all correspondence and documents be sent to him.

There was no further harassment. The realtor forwarded a signed request that we cancel all signed documents. All this torment could as easily have been prevented by way of simple refusal (by the realtor, the title company, other involved attorneys) to give way and sanction to this buyer's unreasonable demands and his disregard of even basic rights and responsibilities.

*It's the whole story of our failures and successes that builds understanding.*

## Chapter 10

# How Hurtful Battles Erupt

The rule, when folks don't live up to our expectations, is to correct our mistaken expectations accordingly. Yet interactions in such encounters don't usually follow this rule. When we speak or act in a way that indicates we're unable or unwilling to comply with another's wishes, the reaction will most likely be a defensive or aggressive attempt to force conformity—and then we're most apt to react defensively or aggressively to such pressure.

This back-and-forth contest can easily turn into hurtful battle. (It's assumed the relationship is important to both parties, or they would simply walk away from such an unpleasant encounter.) As the battle escalates, so does the distress, as we sense the relationship is suffering serious damage. The usual way of stopping the fight is for one participant to give in to the other's expectations. But this leaves one party feeling uncared for and powerless.

As I previously explained, fear and love are the primary emotions that push, pull, and guide us to take better care of protective needs and creative ambitions. But relationships are made up of two or more persons, all with feelings of fear and love pushing and pulling in ways and directions that don't necessarily take into account the other person's limitations and sensitivities. It's necessary to handle disappointments with due consideration of the feelings of all concerned. Battle can't possibly have this result, as is evident in most relationship failures and breakdowns.

## Chapter 11

# *World War II*

I recall the day Pearl Harbor was attacked—the radio reports, newspaper pictures, and conversations of fearful family members and neighbors trying to make some sense of the atrocities. I wasn't yet ten years old, but I felt deeply the horror of the devastation and helplessness. For months, when walking the back roads to and from school and hearing a small plane passing overhead, I instinctively ran for cover. I found no solace in reassurances that war is necessary and that we were safe.

My oldest brother was drafted, though he was handicapped with a type of muscular dystrophy that made it impossible for him to complete even basic training. He was discharged soon after, which left him with a new handicap—a sense of failure and rejection. My next oldest brother tried to enlist, but his application was rejected because of high blood pressure. So no immediate family members went to war. I was grateful.

But my friend who worked in our grocery store was drafted and sent to Germany. He sent me letters and gifts, making it seem that perhaps war wasn't such a terrible thing after all. We knew lots of young men, however, who were killed or sent home with serious injuries or discharged with a crippling condition referred to as "shell shock."

At school, we were taught to knit small squares and sew them together to make "Afghans for Soldiers." (I never met a soldier who ever received one of these covers.) We were taught to plant Victory Gardens, as food shortages were anticipated. Sugar, coffee, meats, shoes, fuels, tires, and more were rationed. Cigarettes and other items were stashed under the counter and saved for regular customers. It became my job to count and paste ration stamps on large official sheets that had to be turned in to wholesale companies along with grocery restocking orders.

The more I've learned about war, the less trust I have in those, on both sides, who declare war. The more I've listened to attempts to justify war and its horrific toll, the more convinced I am that there is no justification for war—though I realize that, when attacked, we have an obligation to defend ourselves, which of course requires killing.

Laura Hillenbrand's book *Unbroken* fell out of the bookshelf (literally) when I was dusting, the day I was writing this story. This book is presented as a World War II story about survival, resilience, and redemption. I was shocked to learn the extremes of brutality human beings practiced in the name of a "just cause." In this book, there is reference to the belief of Japanese warmongers that the Japanese people were the superior race—with an obligation, therefore, to conquer the world and annihilate or enslave all other people.

This book made me see how organized mass destruction is the extreme acting out of out-of-control mishandled fears, and the hold and spread of wrong assumptions that killing the enemy (all people who have remarkably different life views and habits) is essential to self-preservation.

The unfathomable, grievous, vain human error is the all-out global consensus that it's even possible to get rid of inherent human responsibilities (of using powerful emotions to ensure respect and protection of all life) and/or that the outcome of mass killing could possibly be in any way beneficial to anyone.

*Chapter 12*

# *War Cannot Make Peace*

On Memorial Day, I couldn't help thinking about the basic concept of soldiers sacrificing their lives "for the sake of peace," committed to what is assumed to be their duty and the greatest possible contribution to country, family, friends, and God. But the purpose of declaring war is to force compliance with a country's or organization's or individual's preferences, to establish a position of greater power and control. The means is to outsmart, bully, or even kill, if necessary, to subdue and conquer "the enemy."

Whenever we take what we want by way of guile, force, or threat, our opponents suffer loss, injury, and humiliation. So they're surely not at *peace* with us. We've caused them grave suffering. They surely don't truly respect us, a further requirement of peace. We're all aware that peace is defined as "harmony" or "absence of hostility" and that harmony and good will cannot be an outcome of being forced to comply with another's wishes and the sense of loss of rights that results.

War creates a false sense of power on one side and a false sense of powerlessness on the other. Both sides are more vulnerable, provoking even greater fear. Greater fear requires greater effort of self-protection, also not compatible with expectations and promises of peace.

The motivation of war is fear. The motivation of peace is love. Where there is love and sincere caring, even the slightest potential or threat of harm will damage it. Where there is fear there is limited ability for caring, unless feelings of well-being are restored. War, even when it is a necessary response to attack, doesn't achieve this goal, as the dangers of war continue ever present, as do the fears, and on and on.

It's simply not reasonable to expect to ensure or preserve peace or freedom by fighting. Peace and freedom are but vain excuses for engaging in war. Until we openly admit this truth, we're stuck in a place of profound denial of actual potentials for achieving and maintaining peace and freedom.

I realize the terrible price and guilt of admitting this truth. But I also understand the far worse price of ongoing pretense that peace and freedom can result from brutality. It seems we're finally willing to admit that it's always damaging and never helpful to beat up our children, spouses, or next-door neighbors in attempt to force compliance with our preferences. How long will it take to admit it's always damaging and never helpful to beat up folks in other countries, or anyone, in an effort to force compliance with our doctrines and ambitions? Even when our lies and aggression are in reaction to being lied to and attacked, the primary accomplishment is an increase of dishonesty, waste, and destruction in our world, acting contrary to our own doctrines and claims, giving in to and taking on rulership of evil.

## Chapter 13

# *Time Out*

The most difficult writing challenge continues to be finding right words to share what's in my mind and heart on this day and other joyous or troubled days—words that convey my gratefulness for all that's wonderful and sadness for all that's horrible, words that admit my own wounds and failures and related handicaps without compromising best efforts and intentions. I'm hopeful this sharing, if received as intended, will help the reader give serious and open thought to the importance and necessity of not engaging in destructive interaction. Yet there are days when I'm plagued with doubt.

On this particular cool summer day, there's a hint of sun beginning to shine through after a rainy night. I'm downstairs in my fine-art-printing studio at the desk window overlooking a clearing in the woods that surrounds my house. Chipmunks are at play on the walkout concrete deck. A lynx chases a rabbit through the clearing beyond it. Farther out, a crystal-clear river rapids flows down and around boulders and scattered rocky islets. Yet my thoughts settle on a most disturbing recent experience, as described in the next chapter.

## Chapter 14

# The Renter

I'm wondering if I'll ever fully recover from the mistreatment suffered in the course of renting my house in town to a geologist employee of one of the mining companies we fear may destroy our wilderness waterways. This woman was referred to me as an upstanding professional person interested in renting my house. As she recognized its impeccable condition, she gave assurance that she would take good care of it. She offered to take care of snow-removal needs and yard upkeep for a substantial rent reduction. We put together a rental contract that included a statement of respective obligations.

From the beginning, there were multiple complaints. She insisted I must have the carpets cleaned because she smelled dog pee, although my dog wasn't ever allowed in the house. Nonetheless, I had the carpets professionally cleaned. I had the furnace and gas fireplace professionally serviced and plumbing, wiring, and appliances checked out, hoping to discourage further complaints.

But demands continued. All problems turned out to be more a result of misuse than malfunction, especially in regard to a garage door that didn't always respond instantly to the remote's signal. This was an older house with a few typical older-house quirks. Though I made several trips to town from my country home to show this renter how to best handle these quirks, her impatience and unreasonable expectations resulted in ongoing handyman house calls. I took the calls in stride—until the man hired to make these repairs explained he was too frustrated with the renter's demands to continue the job. I hired a garage-door company to take care of the garage door problem, after which there were no further complaints.

*Thoughtful Times*

But at the end of the rental contract, as she was preparing to move out, the renter casually mentioned, "By the way, the garage door hasn't worked for a long time." She wouldn't do the customary walk-through check with me. When I did this check, I found a number of incidents of damage. Custom-made and installed insulated shades had been removed and tossed in a corner of a room above the garage. They were too soiled and wrinkled to refurbish. Without permission, a TV cable had been crudely installed through an outside wall in a room already TV-cable equipped. Stove burner trays were so corroded with burned-on crud they would have to be replaced. The lawn and gardens were overgrown with over-waist-high weeds. I had to employ professional help to restore their pre-rental condition.

The garage door was indeed not working. The owner of the garage-door company hired to make earlier repairs explained that the new damage was such that it couldn't be repaired. He showed me where blunt force, probably from vehicle impact, had caused severe denting inside and out. He assured me these dents were not present when he made earlier repairs.

I explained to the renter why I was withholding the damage deposit. She filed suit against me by way of conciliation court. Despite photographs and witness statements documenting the damages described, and the garage-door company owner's testimony, the judge's decision was "insufficient proof" of damages claimed. The undisputed counter-claim that this renter didn't pay me the contract-required pet-damage deposit or honor her signed agreement to do yard and garden work in exchange for reduced rent wasn't even addressed.

I'm told that my reasons for withholding the damage deposit probably weren't given due consideration because I was unable to attend the hearing. I have a life-threatening sensitivity to formaldehyde products prevalent in old poorly ventilated public buildings. I sent written notice of this handicap to the court, asking if it was possible to have someone appear on my behalf or for me to sit by an open window to minimize risk of allergic reaction. I received no reply. Persons familiar with the poor air quality of this courthouse advised that I should not risk making a personal appearance.

I later learned the renter managed to persuade the man first hired to handle repairs to support her contention that damages to the garage door, making it necessary to replace it, existed prior to her rental. This man admitted writing a letter to this effect at her request. But he wasn't made aware that the door had suffered blunt-force damage after he was no longer involved with repairs.

This renter also managed to enlist the sympathies of the son of another man I hired to plow the driveway of the rented house. She ignored instructions that this gift wasn't intended to take care of all her plowing needs when, late one night, she called this man to insist he must plow her driveway before she had to go to work early the next morning. He was so upset by this rude command that I decided he shouldn't be doing more plowing for her. But after I gave her this message, she sent me an e-mail stating she and this man's son had "worked things out" and he would be doing the plowing for her after all. I let it be because I didn't want to aggravate tension between father and son.

Though I was encouraged to contest the judge's decision, I opted to just pay the renter the amount court-ordered. With this payment was a request for a notarized statement of receipt, as court-ordered. The renter refused to provide this statement. I sent notice of her refusal to the court, along with a request for further instructions, with no response.

It's my experience that a company's key employees' attitudes reflect a company's attitudes. My fear now is that this employee's disregard of agreements and contracts and what is fair and decent treatment, and her devious manipulations that took unfair advantage of kind folks, are evidence of what we should expect as mining companies gut their way through our beautiful country, stripping it of irreplaceable resources, dumping toxic wastes to ruin waterways. We've all heard and read reports of the disastrous impact of metals mining in other states.

I'm thinking we'd best draw up a set of bottom-line requirements for all such companies and their officers—requirement of unmitigated forthright honesty in all transactions, of substantiated due regard for all resources, and of respect for the needs and concerns of all citizens. The penalties for failure to honor these requirements should be so severe as to turn away all but aboveboard companies who openly address and share our concerns.

*Imagine the remarkable benefits for all concerned if powerful companies and their employees practiced truthfulness and kindness.*

## Chapter 15

# *Accidental Cruelty*

My earliest experience of the terrible cost of ignorance occurred when I was three years old, living on a small farm with my parents, my two older brothers, and our farm animals. Our milk cow, Bossy, was my friend. I wasn't permitted to go into the barnyard unless accompanied by my parents, but when I sat on the house side of the fence enclosing the barnyard, Bossy would come to the barn side. I was sure she understood everything I shared with her because every few words, she would respond with a caring moo or grunt. When I put my small fists through the fence openings, she licked them gently as she poked inside for whatever edible morsel I might offer.

Every second Friday, my father went to town to shop for the few food items we didn't produce on the farm. He brought treats home for my brothers and me, usually candies or small cakes. On one occasion, he brought packets of Wrigley chewing gum. I usually shared just a bite of my treat with Bossy, but I didn't really like chewing gum. So, one by one, I unwrapped all five sticks and passed them through the fence to my cow friend.

Late that night I was awakened by my parents' frantic worry that Bossy might die. The veterinarian and my parents were talking about how they couldn't imagine what might have caused her to be so bloated with such terrible spastic abdominal pain. I told them about the chewing gum I gave her. I learned cows can't digest or pass chewing gum. Bossy survived, but if I'd not confessed my terrible mistake, she probably couldn't have been saved.

*Mary Lax*

The hard lesson for me was how easily and innocently we can cause terrible hurt or even death, though our intentions may be entirely caring. This experience also helped my awareness that blame and punishment for accidental harm done can't possibly solve a problem resulting from ignorance. Fortunately, my parents understood this.

## Chapter 16

# *Grandpa*

Probably I was invited for weeklong visits to my grandparents' farm after my parents moved to town because they were aware how much I missed farm life. My grandpa must have understood how impossible it was for me to find happiness in town because he talked with me about how he couldn't imagine ever leaving his farm. But he thought maybe that was because he was old and set in his ways. He promised that, in time, I would find friends and things to do in town that made me happy. I believed him.

I remember clearly the first weeklong visit. The weather was such that I had to bring long underwear. Woodstoves were kept burning, and there were more household chores than usual, such as heating bricks for warming beds at night because bedrooms weren't heated. And chamber pots had to be kept clean, unless we'd rather get dressed and hike through the house yard, and the chicken and geese yard, to the outhouse when we needed a toilet during the night. As it turned out, I was awakened early enough when Grandpa called, "Time to milk the cows," that if I hurried getting ready to go with him, as he expected I should, I'd have plenty time to make a trip to the outhouse.

I had my own milking pail and stool, and my own assigned cow—and I was mighty proud that I could fill my smaller milk bucket almost as quickly as my grandpa filled his larger bucket. He never failed to remind me that he knew no other three-year-old girl who milked a cow so well.

Sometimes he would have me move aside to sit on the sill of the barn doorway so I wouldn't get kicked by cows that showed signs of being disturbed by my presence. Then, to help me not get too bored and restless, every few minutes he'd say "Okay, now open your mouth wide" as he aimed the cow's teat so that, when he squeezed and pulled down, the stream of milk went right into my mouth without a splatter on my face, and we'd laugh with delight over such a silly thing we mastered.

He let me help with all sorts of farm work. I walked with him when he plowed fields with his horse-drawn plow, climbed ladders with him to pick ripe fruit before it dropped to the ground, and turned the handle of the monstrous cream separator as he slowly poured in the whole milk. I even helped rake up manure and lay new straw in the horse stalls.

Oh, how I loved those horses! They were the biggest, most friendly and gentle creatures I've ever known. One, old Nell, was my favorite. Grandpa taught me to ride her bareback. Her enormous body was so broad my legs stuck straight out sideways. She was so tall I couldn't climb on or off her without Grandpa's strong-arm lift.

Whenever I was in the house yard playing, Nell would come to the barnyard side of the fence and wait for me to come pet and talk with her. Grandpa's trust of this great dame was such that, occasionally, he would even let me go into the barnyard with her alone. The worst day of my young life was when we were having our usual visit and old Nell pulled away and fell down to the ground, rolled over, and died. After I learned that her dead body was sold to a factory for making glue, I couldn't stop crying for weeks.

I continued to make these weeklong visits whenever I could until my grandparents had to move to town because they were no longer able to take care of their huge farm. Wonderful memories that continue to give joy and a sense of ever-available support include the widespread well-earned deep regard of all who had the good fortune of knowing my grandpa. I recall his many serious conversations with neighbors and relatives. (He thought it was good that a youngster was interested.) It seemed he felt an urgent need to teach folks about farming, who weren't necessarily eager to learn. He also shared advice about politics, business, and other ordinary human responsibilities of getting along well with one another and living a good life. Eventually he succeeded at persuading fellow farmers to rotate crops and turn some crops back into the soil to keep it healthy; to not let oil-exploration companies destroy great farmland on vain promises of financial wealth; and to give Roosevelt's farm-program proposals careful serious thought. There were ongoing disagreements with my father, his son, on this subject.

He could always make time for following baseball games on his custom-built battery radio, for attending church and making ice cream on Sundays, for reading favorite newspapers, for loving Grandma, and for his grandchildren.

*A child learns best by way of how those in charge*
*handle challenges and responsibilities*
*and how she or he is treated.*

## Chapter 17

# *Harsh Truths We All Must Own*

We've been taught to handle fear by way of all sorts of devious controlling maneuvers. To correct this craziness, we must stop blaming each other for the horrific state of human affairs. We're all seriously handicapped from the moment of birth. Even with the best possible care, guidance, and example from loving parents, none of us is spared the damages of neglect and mistreatment.

We've been taught as well, at least by example, to keep secret the worst offenses suffered and committed, so that it may seem mistreatments aren't as prevalent or serious as I report. But I've worked long and well enough as a therapist to know what the truth is. When and where we can be confident our revelations won't provoke a hurtful reaction, we all have stories of unthinkable neglect and mistreatment to tell. This sharing is necessary to recovery, which in turn is necessary to developing truly effective ways to end neglect and abuse.

*Chapter 18*

# A Bit More Personal History

My earliest memories relate to life on my family's modest farm during the Great Depression. My mother, especially, felt limited by the lack of money and the isolation. When my grandfather, my mother's father, offered to help my parents establish a grocery business in town, they accepted.

I was almost four years old. I missed the country, its freedom, the woods, and the animals. I cried a lot until I found new friends and places to explore. My next-door friend was Tucker, whose mom spanked him every day with switches from their maple tree after stripping him naked. He thought he was whipped because he was the only white kid in his family. One afternoon we found a can of black paint and turned him into a black kid. That good deed almost killed my friend. But his mom did stop spanking him.

My older close friend who worked in our store taught me to dance for customers. I saved the pennies dropped into my pockets when I danced to buy dog food for the neighborhood strays I rounded up and contained in our outhouse—until, after being attacked by frantic beasts when he opened the outhouse door, my dad explained that dogs need to run free. This lecture occurred soon after he explained why I must not dance for customers for money.

There were eventually four brothers, two older, two younger. I took care of my younger brothers when my mother worked in our store. They thought it was fun to tell my parents lies about how I treated them so I would be punished, until my parents realized their tales weren't true. My older brothers thought sisters were for testing the safety of death traps they built for jumping off roofs and leaping over roaring hot trash fires.

Grade-school teachers were especially kind. I was an exceptional student, they said, though I was shy and hardly ever talked. They assigned me roles in plays to show child-development experts I wasn't developmentally or learning handicapped. These great teachers paved the way of an entirely wonderful school experience thereafter.

I even earned a full-tuition music scholarship to a fine university but couldn't come up with room and board money and had to refuse this honor. My parents thought college for girls was wasted unless they didn't intend to get married. I was encouraged (pressured) to enroll in nursing school, a program that back then cost little since we worked full eight-hour shifts in the hospital, evenings or nights, in addition to attending a full schedule of daytime university classes. I graduated as an RN with honors, yet came to realize nursing wasn't the right profession for me. I took a detour into psychiatry, eventually earning degrees in psychology as well as psychiatric nursing.

I married a lawyer. We got along exceptionally well, had seven children, and built a good life together, until my husband became ill with heart disease. My husband, his doctors, our friends and family, and our neighbors all dealt with this terrible misfortune by way of absolute denial.

I awoke one night to find my husband in obvious distress and unresponsive. I knew his doctor wouldn't take seriously my call for help. I ran to a neighbor's house and asked him to make the call. The neighbor decided to first check in with my husband, who by then was fully conscious and claimed he was feeling fine. Together, they concluded it was I who needed help and called the police to escort me to a nearby hospital. I wasn't at all out of touch or out of control. I was very insistent, however, in my efforts to enlist medical help for my husband.

I was literally held prisoner in this hospital on a locked psychiatric ward. Without signed consent, I was forcefully subjected to one after another series of mistreatments—drugs, electric shock, insulin shock—and I was scheduled for a prefrontal lobotomy. Before the day of this scheduled butchering, in the middle of the night, I awoke with a startling mental image of my husband on the floor at home convulsing.

I somehow convinced the night nurse that I must use the phone. Once again, my pleas for help were dismissed as delusional.

But a few moments later my daughter also called my husband's doctor with the same report I had tried to relay. My husband was brought to the same hospital I was at and admitted to intensive care. I wasn't allowed to visit him. When I announced I was leaving the hospital, however, to go home to take care of our children, no one dared to stop me. Not long after this event, my husband died.

There was never an apology by anyone involved in the mistreatments described. Doctors, friends, family members, and neighbors simply avoided me. I was truly alone, with the unbearable pain of abuse suffered, the horrible grief of losing my husband, and the overwhelming challenge of rearing and providing for seven children. Even then I understood that such strong resistance to painful realities had its roots in terrible fear, though I still can't imagine how anyone makes the choice to destroy the messenger rather than admit unwelcome truths.

Still, whenever I talk about this or other hurtful mistreatment, reactions usually turn into attempts to excuse or justify the offenders' misdeeds, often by trying to show that I must have done something to provoke or cause their cruel mistreatment. At times, still, I must shout, *"No!* It's not ever my fault that I'm lied to or about, or not believed, or wrongly accused, or forcefully subjected to horrible punishment!" (And I pray that if or when I cause another such harm, my hurtful words or actions will be as strongly refused.)

This is where corrections must happen before we have reason to expect further improvements in human relationships. No attempts to ignore, deny, belittle, misrepresent, mis-assign, or conceal what is true and important are justified or excusable. Yet I'm sympathetic with all who are plagued by terrible fear—especially as I realize social conditioning favors never admitting such an emotional state. This "holding it in" increases its power. The way to relieve this intolerable burden is to give our fears constructive outlet, to admit fear's hold, and to seek and carry out nondestructive ways of alleviating whatever the threat to well-being happens to be (for example, in the case of serious illness, seeking and providing needed supports and healing intervention).

## Chapter 19

# *Further Thoughts on Differences*

I can't help but wonder how it happened that I've ended up with such an unpopular sense of what's essential to well-being. Some thoughts take me back to childhood influences. Although I strongly objected to what I considered too-restrictive discipline, I came to understand these restrictions represented parental protective effort, referred to by them as "God's will."

Both my parents' families treated all "good" people truthfully and kindly, and shunned all "bad" people. They assumed they were rightful judges as to who was good and who was bad, and that all bad people deserved to suffer, on earth and in hell. When good people suffered great loss and hardship (and mistreatment), however, their misfortune was attributed to "a test of faith in God."

The tendency to judge persons most like them in background, affiliations, and opinions to be good, and persons not like them to be not good, bothered me. But there was little room in my family's thinking for recognizing such an attitude as arrogant and prejudicial.

My different views were stressful to my family, especially since there was no indication of wrongdoing on my part in my unusual thoughts and pursuits. My parents eventually listened as I explained that we don't have to be all-alike to be equally good—that goodness and badness simply define how well or poorly we treat each other and our world. They found no basis of disagreement with this argument, yet they'd never quite concede that their rules were based on fear of whomever and whatever was "different." At least we talked, on occasion, about our disagreements, enough that I'm confident their hearts and minds weren't entirely closed. Possibly we have to experience devastating shocks that strip us naked, utterly without any safe place or hope of protection, to let go completely religious or other biases that are a required part of social upbringing.

## Chapter 20

# *Widowhood*

After my husband died, my search for childcare providers so that I could go back to work full-time was unproductive. The various agencies we expect should assist this search offered every service but what was needed, it seemed. The strongest recommendation was that I should apply for welfare and stay home; yet I was also told I shouldn't be around my children while I was grieving.

One recommended daycare person unloaded my freezer's contents into her boyfriend's truck when he stopped by my house to have lunch with her. Another hired helper was so absorbed in watching soap operas she failed to notice that three of my youngest children were practicing balancing acts on the upstairs porch railing, which frightening situation I walked into as I arrived home from work. A live-in childcare person disappeared one day, without notice, leaving all her possessions behind. We were unable to locate her, even with police involvement.

I replied to the ad of a fourth-year medical student asking to trade household help for room and board. He came for an interview, with excellent references. The plan we worked out looked like my best option and seemed to work well—but years later, I learned he had sexually abused my younger children.

Because my allergy condition has on occasion resulted in near-death systemic failure, the possibility that I might die prematurely, leaving behind seven orphans, was a constant worry. This concern was a major consideration in my consenting to a proposal of marriage from a friend who seemed to truly enjoy our company. We had a great family camping trip through the northeast coastal mountain country and Canada, which led eventually to our moving to that beautiful area.

We weren't at all prepared for the challenges brought on by that move. We bought an old inn overlooking a huge lake. By the following winter, we still didn't have working heat or plumbing, and outside walls were stripped of inside covering awaiting insulation. Money was scarce. Hardships took a heavy toll on family relationships, with the result being the breakup of this second marriage. By then, there was an eighth child.

I couldn't imagine how I would find a way out of that worst-ever situation. There were times when I had to retreat to a place of solitude to hang on to my own good sense. It was during one of these retreats that I felt a loud pop in my head, like a cork released from a champagne bottle. At first, I was frightened. Then I sensed a friendly presence in the room—invisible, but not an ordinary ghost. This presence told the story of its origin, a place no longer recognized in the Far East. Its mission was to guide the way to desperately needed employment opportunities and friendships.

The next week I met a woman, a therapist. We talked about our respective situations. She was head nurse at a university psychiatric hospital. She offered me a job, which turned out to be my first step toward recovery. We moved again when I was offered a better job at an outpatient clinic. Finally, we were able to reclaim a sense of well-being—for the next several years at least.

*Most single-moms are severely handicapped*
*by harsh misjudgments and lack of essential supports.*

*Chapter 21*

# Further Insights in Regard to Close Personal Relationships

I recall no dreadful destructive interactions within my birth family. There was mostly up-front respect of each other's likenesses and differences, with open expressions of fear and love—but also, on occasion, loud stressful disagreements as to how likenesses and differences, and fear and love, ought to be given due consideration. For the most part, necessary adjustments were worked out to the satisfaction of all concerned, as though it was understood that, unless everyone's needs and ambitions were duly honored, no one's needs and ambitions could be well attended.

I naturally expected this same regard in relationships outside my family, which too often didn't happen. In due time, I came to understand why my parents were inclined to be overly protective and realized I was fortunate to have had that caring.

My first husband and I were respectful of each other's likenesses and differences as well, and mostly considerate of respective efforts in handling fear and love, and in attending personal needs and ambitions. But we weren't at all well equipped to handle the devastating fear of dying and losing each other way too soon.

It's this realization that still haunts me. I've come to understand how the overwhelming power of the fear of losing each other reflects the importance of committed relationship to social as well as personal well-being, and how the power of loneliness, when we lose or can't find a suitable life partner, is a further measure of the importance of this essential relationship. But what do we do when right opportunities or prospects of committed relationship are simply nonexistent?

I learned from my short-lived second marriage that the harsh realities of an unusually difficult life situation, no matter how undeserved and devastating, must simply be accepted and dealt with, truthfully and kindly. I learned from this marriage, as well, to heed the advice of a few good friends who wanted to spare me the agony of this attempt at wholeness and warned, "The only man who'd marry a woman with seven young children is either a fool or a saint, and neither makes a very good husband."

Some of the love stories in this book are reports of rather unusual ways of handling loneliness, without resorting to the desperate acting out of its torments. Some of these stories refer to more ordinary vital connections. All these love stories show what happens when we make good use of whatever opportunities there are to share respective gifts and needs, with no vain expectations of or hold on each other.

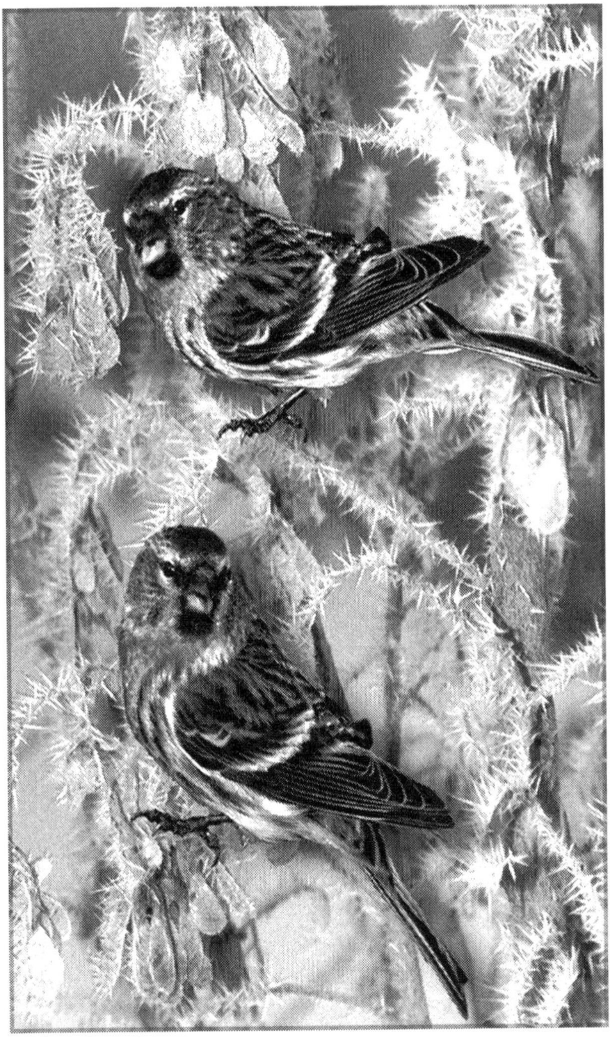

Friends

Share whatever stirs inside us
Learn and teach each other's truths
Unveil potentials that lie hidden
Unwrap gifts that aren't for giving

Reflect our pleasures, passions, dependencies
Encourage and support our aliveness
Celebrate each other's uniqueness
Weep and heal together

Embrace aloneness, without loneliness
Hold hands with pride and gratitude
Walk side by side wherever each or both must go
Have no set end or goal within firm grasp

Join all beauty, starve all evil
Promise only truthfulness and kindness
Have no other laws or ties between us
Have no need of bindings

Give chance and reason for becoming 'US'
Share freely without neglect of Self
Enjoy our lives completely

*Chapter 22*

# A Wonderful Friendship

I was living alone in far north wilderness country, slowly recovering from major surgery and a number of other horrible shocks, fearful my weakened body and tormented soul might not make it through the winter ahead. I was well outfitted with computer connections to anywhere anyone might need or want to go. I did an online search for someone in similar straits who might feel a similar need of human connection.

The guy this search crossed paths with was recovering from the prolonged illness and death of his second wife and a number of other horrible life shocks. He feared that his broken heart and bitter outlook might succeed at pushing him to end his life. We rather easily decided he should drive the four-hundred-plus miles to my place for a visit.

But that visit didn't happen the way we intended. One night, when this new friend was trying to reach me from his home by phone, he became concerned when I didn't answer and made the long trip to my home that night. By the time he arrived, I was unresponsive. When I regained consciousness in the hospital, I learned I had a bad case of flu and had suffered a severe systemic allergic reaction, possibly to the flu virus itself.

As already noted, this peculiar allergy condition has been a major health issue for me since birth. At times, I can prevent life-threatening reactions by careful avoidance of triggers and/or with medication. At other times, nothing seems effective. The condition is such that I can't go into most public buildings without getting sick. This new friend eventually took on the job of shopping for me.

*Thoughtful Times*

Our next visit went more the way we intended. My dog and cat and I greeted my most welcome friend as he got out of his car, with instant buddy-ship all round. As we shook hands, he remarked how it was a good thing he came when he did, for already he'd noted assorted "haphazards" begging his expert attention, and he was sure there were some mighty fine fish in the river down below. Wasn't it fortunate he'd brought his fishing pole and hip boots?

We didn't get much fishing or other work done that day or night. We had too much to talk about. By the end of the day I sensed that, if we were to get along, he'd have to make a few changes in his opinions as to what is and isn't a woman's privilege and work. (I don't think he ever did get this quite straight.) He enjoyed my cooking, the crackling wood-stove fire, the other comforts and amenities of my small rough-built house, and our conversations that went on way past dark. When I mentioned bedtime, he offered to sleep on the couch with my dog and cat.

By the time this gentleman headed back to his home, most all the haphazards he had made note of were taken care of, and my freezer was well stocked with small mouth bass. We even made a plan for me to visit him, and for his next visit to my place. We continued this back-and-forth sharing of our respective homes, life habits, and interests for years. We'd spend a week or more at my house, then a week or more at his house. When at my house, he helped with whatever projects I had going; when at his house, I helped with his projects. (We both had too much we thought we had to do, always.)

We both worked as professional photographers. Explorations of my and his worlds with cameras in hand were especially enjoyable. There was always lots of learning and teaching with each other. For the most part, these exchanges happened without great effort. But on occasion, this devoted friend would take charge and insist I let him show me how to do something his way. I too, on occasion, insisted on doing a job my way.

I'm remembering the time this ordinarily friendly struggle ended in hurtful interaction—which eventually caused both of us to realize how important it is to give great care to respecting each other's tender places. This exceptionally skilled and caring man was helping me lay a looped carpet, insisting we should drill holes through the edging trim, the carpet, and the underneath flooring all together before applying screws to hold it all in place.

My preference was to make these holes with a hammer and small nails, as I was fearful the drill bit might get tangled in the carpet loops. My friend's way prevailed. As I feared, the drill got caught in the carpet loops, pulling out a couple of long rows before he realized what was happening and could turn off the drill. I was yelling something that he must have heard as "I told you so." Both of us were crushed by this harsh exchange.

My friend fled the scene, probably the best possible move at the time. I was left to clean up the mess. Cleaning up other folks' messes is high on my list of few but absolute intolerances. It took a long time and considerable work to reclaim peace.

Through all the years we were best buddies, there was but one other incidence of hurtful interaction. We decided to take both our cars on one trip from my house to his. My car was a Jeep Wrangler, without room enough for both of us with our gear, a large dog and cat and their essentials, plus items we wanted to transport from my home to my friend's home or back to mine. We were putting too many miles on his van. We anticipated times when our respective commitments would make it difficult for us to make every trip together.

Long-distance driving is a challenge for me. I can't safely drive at night. I have what's in lay terms called a wrinkled retina in one eye, which severely limits depth perception. I have to plan trips to assure ample daylight and not much heavy traffic. I also have to take into account my allergy to formaldehyde-related products like room fresheners and sprays, which are heavily used in public bathrooms and motels.

Our departure time was delayed. Traffic was heavier than anticipated, and we had to make extra stops for my elderly cat. It was already too dark for me to drive when we were still forty miles from our destination. I had to pull over onto the highway shoulder and stop. My friend was upset with me, insisting I had to keep going. He was shouting how and why we couldn't stop there. I gave in out of desperation and got back onto the highway, driving no more than fifteen miles an hour, praying out loud for guidance.

We made it without terrible incident, thanks I'm sure to the helping hand of some higher power. My friend eventually admitted he assumed that when I said, "I stopped because I couldn't see where I was going," that it was simply very difficult, as opposed to impossible, for me to see well enough to drive.

In the course of working our way through this struggle, we both came to realize the importance of taking literally all information provided by each other as to our respective limitations and disabilities, as well as our strengths and talents. It also became clear that this honesty with each other wouldn't be possible if we weren't truthful with ourselves. That's how we came to understand it's this up-front awareness and acceptance of ourselves that's the key to trust in any relationship. Only if and when we correct failures to determine and take care of our own human belongings can we rightly expect to be able to have good relations with others.

My friend died recently. His doing my shopping and other generous deeds were truly great gifts of this relationship. I miss all this help terribly, but it's knowing that I'll not ever feel the pure joy again of his turning into my driveway, or his tight hugs, or the enormous caring reflected in his deep blue eyes, or his taking my hand when I was feeling hurt or scared or unsteady, that's unbearable.

When we met, and for several years after, I lived in a house I built myself that overlooked a great river. This house had a few structural handicaps that made care more demanding than I could manage as I lost physical strength and agility. I was feeling more and more isolated, generally, as my eyesight and allergy problems grew worse. I was reluctantly preparing to make the dreaded big move.

At first, the best all-round option seemed to be to move closer to my friend's home. Though we had considered sharing a home, we both concluded separate housing best suited our respective habits and obligations. We did a rather intensive search for a house near his that suited my needs and means. We found nothing suitable that I could afford. Meanwhile, I was becoming acquainted with a community well known for its appeal to artists and its art events. I made a number of visits, checking out the potential for expanding my fine-art reproduction business. In due time, I did sell my river home and buy a house in this small town. My friend was entirely supportive of this move and provided much-needed help in the middle of a bitter winter.

He continued to make frequent visits and to be a vital participant in my life. He even became involved in my art repro business. We turned a number of his and my wildlife photos into large canvas prints, which became popular. This business grew as I'd hoped it would, leaving little time for trips to my friend's house. But he seemed to truly enjoy all the opportunities and offerings of the new community—fishing, photography, interesting folks, great stores, and all kinds of adventures. Living in town was at first great fun and necessary to building my business, but my allergy condition became more and more troublesome, with frequent emergency-room ordeals. Various home improvements helped, but not enough.

When my older brother died, leaving me a tidy sum of money, I decided to use this unexpected inheritance to build a toxin-free wilderness cabin. My friend encouraged this decision, I think mostly because he realized how much happier and healthier I was when I was living in the country. My sons and daughters were supportive as well, and even became involved in selecting the building site and drawing up plans. My friend and my sons seemed to think they should take charge of various negotiations with builders. By the time the cabin was finished, we all felt quite proud of a job well done.

We had much to celebrate, especially as my allergy condition improved remarkably.

Even as my friend and I became less and less able to do all that we intended to do here, we still enjoyed the simple lifestyle of this beautiful place and easy open friendship with each other. An especially wonderful time was his last visit with his son, who drove thousands of miles to have one last week of talk and fishing with his dad.

## Chapter 23

# *Life Is Good*

There have been several major relocations during my life, primarily for survival reasons. I'm remembering the move after the breakup of my second marriage, to accept the job that came by way of the out-of-the-blue ghost encounter. The Cape Cod house I contracted to purchase was close to the main part of town, on a steep hill overlooking the neighborhood below.

As is my homemaker's habit, I foresaw all kinds of possibilities for turning this modest house and yard into a wonderful family home. On the way to the trash dump, I had noticed piles of old used brick I was sure would make a great patio along the very edge of the property—the edge that dropped sharply to the busy street below. Two large old trees were spaced right for securing a hammock, though this arrangement might let the hammock swing far enough beyond that edge to create a rather high-risk situation. (We'd have to post rules of precaution.)

Fencing, here and there, would provide climbing space for peas and cucumbers and such. I'd use the small lower branches trimmed from the two hammock trees for tomato-plant stakes along the opposite property boundary beyond the turn-around drive. Inside improvements would include enlarging the dining area by moving a wall to accommodate our eight-foot-long mahogany trestle table and benches. We'd have to convert part of the basement into extra bedroom space, and there was lots of scrubbing and painting to do.

We weren't all that surprised that, immediately, we became objects of neighborhood curiosity and speculation. A single mom and eight active kids, accustomed to doing whatever needs doing to make a good life for all of us, understandably attracts undue attention, but we couldn't possibly have anticipated some wonderful things that "just happened."

After a vigilant neighbor took great care to inform me that I shouldn't expect anything to grow in that yard's poor soil, the small branches I stuck into the ground for tomato-plant stakes took root and grew leaves. This neighbor was sure I must practice witchcraft, especially as he noticed that my car license plate lettering spelled TAROT. An abundance of garden produce let us share leftover fruits and vegetables with him and other neighbors. So much was going on with my kids and their friends, and my friends and clients, that neighbors complained that they weren't given notice of missed events.

The event of the season was a patio cocktail party, attended by far more folks than were invited, that became the talk of the town. Fortunately, no one fell out of the hammock down to the street below. A guest reported that the steep hillside had been the town dump many years ago, after which one son initiated an excavation project that produced more artifacts than could possibly fit in our house. He distributed these prizes among appreciative neighbors.

Our Golden Lab dog, a working co-therapist, accidentally mated with a neighbor's Saint Bernard, producing seven puppies so cute and lovable that people begged to adopt them. When I painted the outside of the house and was high up the ladder working way too close to the main electrical wires or on the steep roof hanging onto dormers, folks came out of nowhere to my rescue. Several years later, when we had to make another big move, hundreds of near and far neighbors came to our garage sale, bought everything, and wept over our leaving.

This remarkable recovery ended abruptly and painfully, without warning. But before I get too far into that dreadful story, I want to share several special friendships. Remembering these unusual pure and simple connections has helped pull me through the worst life experiences, when there was no one and nothing else to trust.

*Chapter 24*

# *Another Fisherman Friend*

He fished year-round on a huge deep lake—the front yard of a rustic upscale restaurant where I worked as hostess, bartender, and piano player. He told stories of encounters with lake inhabitants and storms, and related heroic survival feats. I submitted one of these stories, about his adventures with a sea monster, complete with photos of this ancient uncombed white-haired and bearded toothless storyteller, to a nearby city newspaper. It was published on the front page.

Suddenly this gentleman was enjoying the benefits and suffering the harassments of fame. He invited me to his house to share a cup of coffee. I teased him about the stack of newspapers he had secretly purchased and stashed away in what surely was the only empty corner of his disorderly living space. He admitted to feeling plagued by loneliness; fame was exciting but otherwise didn't help much. He talked about why he never married, his father's early accidental death, his mother's prolonged illness and death from cancer, their poverty, his drunkenness. And he confessed, with a chuckle, that some of his wild adventure stories were made up.

We walked through his huge well-kept garden as he explained its success was from all the fish bones and innards he buried all around. Later he showed me how to clean and bone small lake perch as he instructed me to never let water touch dead fish until I'm ready to cook them. "Just remove their heads, guts, and bones and throw them into a freezer bag," he stressed.

The next day, he hitched a ride to make the four-mile trip from his house to mine, with at least a dozen bags of lake perch ready to put in my freezer and boxes of fresh produce from his garden. As we carried this bounty from his friend's truck into my kitchen, he announced they'd be staying for supper. This exchange turned into a weekly ritual.

He never ran out of stories, but he did learn to give warning as to which were "gospel truth" and which were "just for fun." As I realized how dependent he was on kind folks for rides to and from the lake, and how much he looked forward to these brief encounters, I often invited him to accompany me on longer trips, for making client house calls throughout this rural mountainous country. He knew the history of this entire region and its families, and he guided me through back-road wilderness I would have become lost in otherwise.

In turn, I accidentally introduced him to pleasures he otherwise would never have experienced like lunch at McDonald's. Without giving much thought to his food habits, on one trip as we came upon a McDonald's drive-in about lunchtime, I offered to treat him to a meal and asked what he would like. His response was, "I don't know anything about their food. Whatever you're having is fine." We ended up with milkshakes, burgers, and fries.

I noticed he watched closely how I unwrapped and handled the food and utensils, and copied my every move. As we finished eating and wiped our hands and faces and disposed of the mess, he said, "Well, I think that may be the best lunch I've ever had." Every time we did one of those trips after this, his request was, "Would it be not too much trouble to make sure we're near a McDonald's at lunchtime?" (We weren't aware, at the time, that this food isn't healthy.)

This gentleman became family. When I moved to the far side of the neighboring state because of a great job offer, the sense of loss was huge. We talked on the phone, but phone visits were difficult because of his hearing problem.

Late one day, as I was driving through town on my way home from work, I noticed an uncombed white-haired and bearded man with a small strapped-together suitcase standing at a street crossing, appearing to be waiting for a ride. I stopped. Yes, this man was my old friend. "What on earth are you doing here?" I asked.

He explained, "I hired a guy to drive me here. I didn't know your address, so I had him drop me off in the center of town, expecting you'd drive by here sooner or later." I think he would have stayed longer than the two-week visit we all mostly enjoyed. But my daughters were anxious to have their bedroom back, and we couldn't think of a kind way to insist that he take a bath and let us launder his one suit of clothing. I offered to drive him back to his home.

*Note how, in all these love stories, the only*
*outstanding essential ingredient*
*is mutual trust that can only develop from truthfulness and kindness.*

*Chapter 25*

# *Summer People*

It's commonly assumed that when wealthy, prominent, big-city families vacation in lush idyllic country, native residents who cater to the needs and desires of these visitors will take on attitudes of servitude, and the visitors will take on attitudes of superiority. But that's not how it was in the lakeside restaurant where I worked.

Most of our customers spent the entire summer in lakeshore cabins their families had owned for several generations—folks who were well-known and respected writers, artists, educators, musicians, and corporate heads. Some restaurant staff had comparable backgrounds. The owners and I, and a few other staff members, were well established professionally. So possibly it wasn't remarkable that these gatherings turned into occasions of learning and teaching for all of us.

We of course carried out our respective service/customer roles with serious dedication until all primary functions were fulfilled. Then, often through much of the night, there was the kind of heartfelt generous hungry exchange of experiences and observations I've since wished would happen throughout the world. There was no felt urge or need to compete with, or make judgments about, each other's widely differing views—or justify our own.

Even more reassuring was how openly and easily we talked about the pain and horror that accompanies awareness of gross waste and disregard for our planet and its inhabitants and resources, and what we each and all must do to help stop such crimes.

If this were the usual way intelligent caring folks interacted instead of the exception, I'm confident we would correct horrendous human misdeeds and end the suffering from and the fighting over failures and mistakes.

*Chapter 26*

# The Fire Chief and the Fortune Teller

Kept well-guarded by the village fire chief's usual tough-guy front were wonderful sensitive caring attributes that he seemed oddly comfortable sharing with me. I think he must have sensed my more sophisticated demeanor was designed to protect my tender places.

We talked about everything, once we had checked out each other's trustworthiness. His routine was to stop by the restaurant where I worked during quiet midafternoon breaks. He'd order a draft beer and a Reuben sandwich, admit to feeling kind of down, and complain about recent social, political, or personal debacles. In turn, I'd confess my latest disturbing encounters and worries, and he'd lend support. Usually, after not more than half an hour, we'd wander off this conversation track to talk about larger regrets and wishes.

This guy had jobs other than fire chief. He drove the snowplow and the road grader, and he was running for election to the school board. One day I admitted a fascination with huge workhorse machines and mentioned I'd welcome an invitation to ride with him when he was plowing or grading, or even rushing to a fire. One bleak stormy day he stopped with his plow in front of my house and yelled, "Okay! Get in!" After issuing a few basic instructions and showing me how to raise and lower the plow blade and adjust its angle, he stopped, got out, and directed me to move over to the driver's seat—and I drove the snowplow.

I was pleased and proud to have had this experience and to have such an obliging friend. Since this man was a committed husband and dad when he wasn't plowing, grading, fighting fires, commiserating with me about world troubles, or teaching me to handle large equipment, we had to contend with occasional raised eyebrows. We talked about this problem. He assured me his family was aware of our visits, trusted that our friendship was just that, and understood the importance of outside alliances that give healthy respite from daily disappointments and frustrations.

I did eventually get to ride with him in the fire truck and even help care for victims rescued from their burning home. For that privilege, I was awarded a gold lapel pin with "honorary volunteer fire-department member" engraved on it.

A woman who also was not overly concerned with unduly restrictive relationship attitudes dropped by to join my conversations with the fire chief. During the second such visit, she announced that she had psychic abilities, as did most of her family going way back. She said she was "picking up" certain spirit activities and revelations she thought we should be made aware of. Since she referred to occurrences in our respective lives that we'd not talked about with anyone, we were quite impressed. The spirit informants' advice she offered proved to be most helpful. We looked forward to her counsel and to learning more about her interests.

This woman was sure I had psychic abilities also and urged me to give time and thought to developing these abilities. She even offered to be my teacher and guide, yet she easily accepted my explanation that I was sure I'd best give my efforts to learning to better handle the here-and-now requirements of this world.

She invited me to meet her family of a half-dozen young children, unusually well-mannered and informed. The older youngsters took care of the babies when she worked nights. Her husband was prone to disappearing for weeks at a time to attend to his spiritual pursuits. Their home was orderly with few furnishings. Wide, deep windowsills were filled with seedlings waiting for warmer weather to be moved to outdoor gardens.

I learned much from this family. I especially appreciated the matter of fact way they handled health handicaps, hateful misjudgments, and gossip related to their unusual interests and habits.

## Chapter 27

# *My Mom*

In sharing this story, I'm stepping outside of my book-writing guidelines—carefully established to spare my sons and daughters embarrassment—but this story is such a perfect example of how the sheer innocence, love, and honesty of children too easily become fuel for the fires of hateful prejudice that I'm feeling I must include it. (Please, dear son, forgive me.)

My son was in first grade. School wasn't an easy adjustment for a boy who must "show and tell" whatever's in his heart and soul, no matter the occasion or protocol. This story's occasion was Parent-Teacher Night. For this special event, students were asked to write stories about their mothers to be displayed for all to see and read. The teacher suggested they might want to include a drawing and a few sentences about what their mothers do that they especially appreciate.

My son was so excited to have me meet his teacher and his friends' mothers and read his story that I knew I must attend this meeting. I also knew it would be difficult to find someone to replace me at the restaurant where I worked.

Though all the difficulties were worked out, I was late. When I walked into the classroom, feeling a bit out of place in my rather dressy work attire, I noticed a group of parents in a cluster studying one story posted in a prominent space. I walked in that direction. It was my son's story they were viewing so intensely. Greetings weren't friendly. All moved away without comment, in fact. Body language oozed disdain.

I noticed the paper my son used for his story was larger than the rest. He had taped two sheets together lengthwise to be able to draw a tall, glamorous figure with tousled curly hair, long jeweled earrings, fancy bracelets, and a kind of sexy pose. (I'm not tall and don't wear much jewelry or have curly hair.)

I was feeling a bit scared to read the story that went with this drawing, especially with everyone in the room still staring at me. I moved around the room, viewing other drawings and stories about mothers in aprons, with hair done in braids and buns, who were baking cookies and cakes and doing ironing and such, kind of wishing I was one of them. As I dared embrace my son's masterpiece, I read:

*MY MOM!*
*She's beautiful!*
*She makes drinks and plays piano and makes people happy.*
*She's everybody's best friend.*
*She likes men!*
*I'm really glad she's my mom!*

He had obviously had help with spelling and punctuation.

I was all too aware that if looks and vibes could kill, I'd be dead, which left me feeling sad. But I wondered if at least a few of these moms secretly wished their sons carried similar outrageous impressions and appreciation of them. Mostly, though, I wanted to shout, "And I'm really glad he's my son!"

## Chapter 28

# *Insistent Calls from Behind*

He was a psychiatrist and my boss at an inpatient hospital. He supervised my work with primary therapy patients. He didn't say much during supervision sessions or even during full staff–patient review meetings.

Occasionally he scribbled brief comments in the margins of patient notes—"I don't get it!" or "I still don't understand what you're doing with your patients." I gave greater thought and care to making notations that I hoped would be easier to understand. Otherwise, since I received no worse objections, I assumed all was well.

Early one morning, walking along the hospital corridor, I heard this doctor call out from some distance behind me, "Hey, Lax, wait up!" I stopped and waited. We walked together quietly for a few dozen steps before he said, "I still don't have a clue as to what you do with your patients. But I do observe, whatever it is, it's working better than anything else that's happening here, so for God's sake do more of it!"

Years later, long after I left this position, I received a handwritten invitation to a housewarming from this doctor's wife. I felt so honored I rearranged my life to be able to make the long trip to attend this event.

The new house was modern and efficiently laid out, with unusual placement of appliances and simple efficient furnishings, as might be expected in the home of a person physically handicapped. There were fewer guests than I anticipated, and the doctor wasn't present. His wife and other guests were friendly, yet I felt rather out of place. I hadn't previously met anyone there and wondered why I was the only guest from the hospital where I had worked with this doctor.

I jumped in reaction to a commanding call from behind, "Hey, Lax, you must be wondering why you're here. Well, I want to talk with you about a cruel personal blow—I'm losing my sight!" He left no room for me to offer condolence as he continued, "I think I've figured out what you do with patients—you know about the pain and fear that grab control when we suffer worst life challenges. You know the help we need to get through the grief, back to a place of caring."

We found a quiet corner and sat together on the floor, lotus style. We talked through most of the night. We wiped each other's tears. We hugged. I drove home. We've not been together since, though I've heard from time to time that he's doing well.

*Chapter 29*

# The End of My World

I was summoned to the clinic director's office. "You're to take a leave of absence until further notice, starting now," the director announced. "This is unrelated to your work, which is exemplary. You'll continue to receive full salary. Don't question or talk with anyone about this. You'll trust this action is in our and your best interests."

I couldn't quietly give in to this outrageous order. In effect, I assumed a position of battle, as I did "talk about this." Coworkers took sides. In a sense, my side won the war, and I was allowed to return to work, but by then there was too much hurt on both sides. A number of us resigned. I opened a private practice, bartering with clients who couldn't afford private fees—a remarkable experience. For a while, all seemed well again.

Then came a series of overt aggressions. Hateful posters were tacked to my house and garage. My car tires were slashed repeatedly. Phone conversations were intercepted, and I received anonymous life threats. Persons unknown tormented my children with vicious accusations against our family. They were even physically attacked for no reason. I accidentally learned a private investigator had been hired to find dirt to be used to destroy the high regard I enjoyed among peers and in the community. Accusations of mental illness and pacts with the devil contributed to my terror.

I traveled well out of town to find a colleague to share this account with and to ask advice, half expecting the recommendation would be medication. But the response was, "You've gotten too close to someone's terrible secret. The torments won't stop, I'm sure, until or unless you leave the area or you're dead." I tried to ignore this advice—until the attacks were directed at my clients as well. So I had to accept, once again, that I must simply walk away from an intolerable situation.

A lawyer friend continued to investigate long after I left this community. She eventually learned that it all started with pressure put on the mental-health clinic's director by a powerful evil man who was afraid I'd learned about his drug smuggling crimes from clients who worked for him.

I had not been so informed.

*Chapter 30*

# *Life after Death*

A friend offered his wilderness property on a river way up north as a retreat for recovering life trust and purpose. Another friend gave me a book: *The Second Half of Life* by Angeles Arrien. The first words I read in this book were, "To live like a river flows, carried by the surprise of its own unfolding, when the gift of wisdom emerges and reveals itself." I took these words to mean my friend's wilderness river retreat was where I needed to go.

That river and the ten-acre plot it flowed through required and showed the ways of clean bold habits and structures that began to take form the moment I first walked its banks, as it offered the sanctuary I needed for healing. It was there that I learned how life's smells, sounds, hues, tempers, and labors cause and are caused by harsh demands and generous bounties of the seasons and each day's ordinary and uncommon moods and rituals. It proved that there are no set rules or other means for measuring right and wrong feelings, thoughts and needs, or good and bad rains and winds and fires, or the gains or losses they leave or take. It showed that there are no good rules for moving with, away from, against, or despite life disasters, duties, and gifts. The right way is coexistence and cooperation.

The friend who took me to this place for healing decided to stay with me as he realized the depth and powerful hold of grief's grip. He somehow knew to wrap me in his stout arms as the demons ripped through me, body and soul.

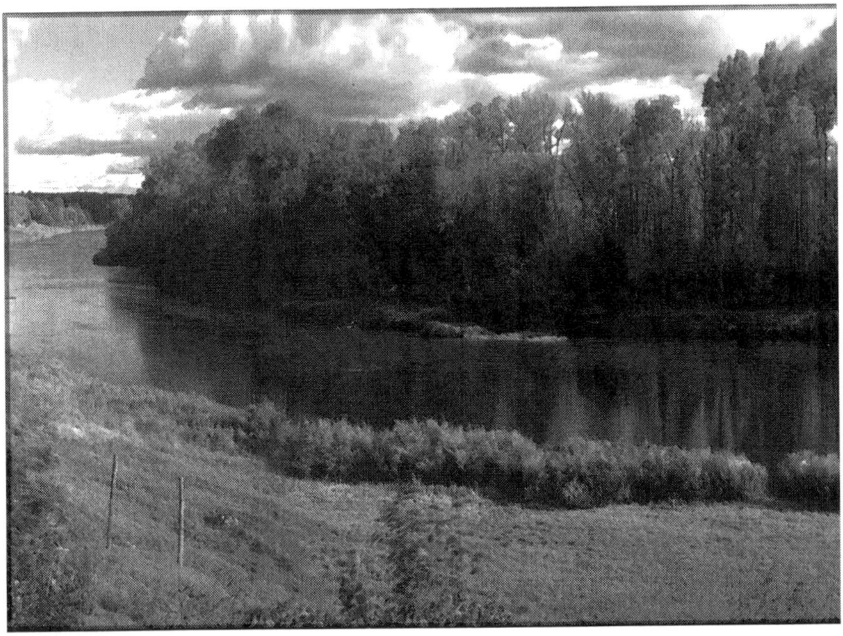

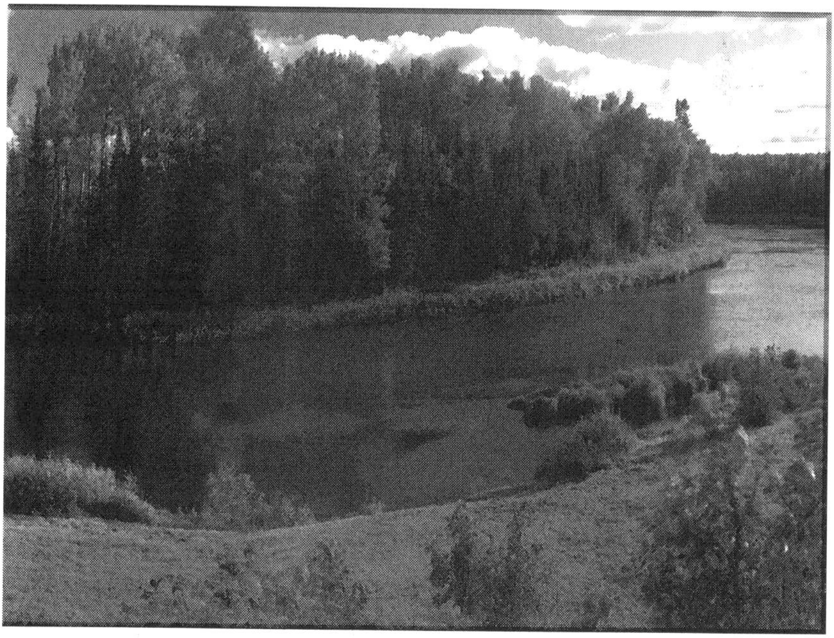

*Chapter 31*

# Re-Birthing

Our shelter was a small travel trailer. As the snow melted, the rains poured every day through June. I made lots of trips through the day and night down and back up the steep slippery clay riverbank. This ritual journey became as essential to recovery as the wailing of unbearable grief.

The sun returned, the birds sang, buds burst open. The owner of this place of refuge and I drew plans to build a cabin and started digging to lay the foundation. I went back east to sell my house there and gather belongings. Another friend and my youngest son drove back to this new homestead with me.

*Thoughtful Times*

As we arrived at the river property, the first thing we saw was a backhoe perched precariously halfway down the steep slope overlooking the river. The operator was yelling that he'd have to make a road to dig the rest of the twelve-foot-deep trench to the river for laying the pipe to bring up water. A storm was building in the west. We all pitched in to get this job done. About ten feet from the river's edge, we noticed a kink in the pipe that would have to be cut out and the pipe spliced. We'd have to drive over fifteen miles to town for a connector. I let the backhoe go, thinking we'd finish filling the trench by hand. (Two years later, we were still dumping wheelbarrows of dirt into this trench.)

By winter, the cabin was livable, though surely not finished. Savings were spent, with no job in sight. Hardships were such that both friends decided to move on. My son had moved out to attend college. It was a brutal winter, with much to cause and give room and purpose to profound realizations.

The entire experience of establishing this homestead, surviving mostly by way of my own wits and labor, was truly a rebirthing. Never again could I fail to give myself due credit for my accomplishments or own my mistakes. (The whole story of this recovery needs its own book, which I may write someday.)

When not out scavenging for firewood and food, I spent eerie winter days and nights drawing and tagging simple diagrams showing causes and mechanics of human suffering. This project helped me hang on to the few threads of hope and good will this work reawakened.

I'm including parts of this study with these stories. Though representations are somewhat different from current efforts to give human failures and needed corrections useful reference, I'm thinking this shift in perspective may help "seeing" how improvements in handling fear and love, and rules requiring truthfulness and kindness, are crucial to ending violence.

It's my contention that if and when each and all of us do the hard work of giving due attention to and report of personal observations and experiences, we'll realize that it's truly by way of fitting together these different pieces of truth that we'll better understand the importance of each and all of those pieces, and each and all of us.

For example: Yesterday a friend sent me a copy of an article she thought noteworthy that describes a recent discovery that persons with certain chromosome variations are more prone to depression than others. The assumption is that those chromosome variations may well be a cause of depression, and that if we find or develop a way to alter the deviant chromosomes to be more "normal," we can better treat this illness.

My view is that this thinking is far too restrictive—it represents yet another attempt to undo human problems by way of undoing human differences. I can't help but wonder why we still don't admit that human differences may not need to or be able to be "fixed," or even why we assume depression should or can be eliminated. It's my experience and understanding that feelings of depression serve to enlist our attention to whatever vital ways we're not taking good care of ourselves and our lives. We must determine the failure and how to correct it.

I've proved this to be true in the course of helping hundreds of depressed clients of all ages and circumstance. I've even worked with groups of clinically depressed persons thought to have physiological need of potent antidepressants who learned to better attend to their mental health through helping each other define neglected needs and ambitions, and ways to better take care of these responsibilities. I'm wishing the scientists examining human chromosomes might include this discovery in their studies.

This seems a good place to mention that, whenever I've been able to enlist participation in open discussion about "What are you afraid of?" and "What do you think is the best possible way to take care of that fear?" invariably a nonviolent "right thing to do" is worked out. Children, especially, do this sharing rather easily, which gives great hope, but strongly suggests that as children we're actually taught not to use this natural problem-solving ability.

There are days, still, when I must accept that all I can do is give my best effort to making sure overwhelming painful memories, grief, and doubts are all kept in their right place. The image is that of keeping a candle burning. Though few will notice its light and warmth or realize the terrible costs and struggles of keeping its flame from being extinguished, I'm responsible, still, for making sure it doesn't die or give off poisonous gasses.

I watch a chickadee clinging to a suet ball on the tree outside my window and marvel at how this small, fragile creature survives the minus-forty-degree cold. I rescue a woodpecker that came to dine too early, whose body heat melted the icy suet enough that he became its prisoner as the moisture refroze. He seemed to know I'd come to his aid.

## Chapter 32

# Circles, Triangles, Squares

I often use simple drawings to assist "seeing" how the many segments of information collected about human problems and dysfunctions fit together. Keep in mind that every thought we send out or take in, every action directed by or at us, is a seed of health or sickness that grows into a plant that flowers, bears fruit and new seeds, depending on how well or how poorly it's sowed, fed, protected, and harvested.

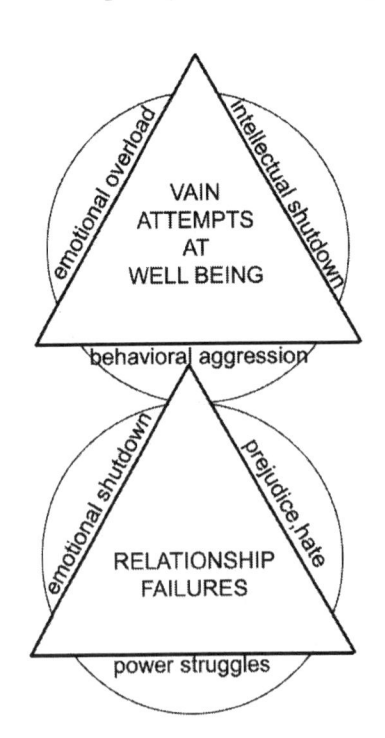

The diagram of interactive themes shows the prevalence and sanction of thoughts and acts that are antagonistic to life—the overload of fear, grief, and guilt; the desperate survival attempts to break free of or overcome unattended life needs and limitations; the resistance to admitting the damages. Complete breakdown is inevitable if we don't realign emotional, intellectual, and physical powers within the constructs of the life circle.

I find geometric symbols helpful in representing and cleaning up ideas. I didn't realize when I began using this aid to objective thinking that the use of symbols is common in ancient studies.

An *I Ching* passage seems especially relevant to my own discoveries.

I quote: "The symbol of the greatness of heaven is the circle, and that of the earth is the square. Movement in a straight line is a quality of magnitude and of the creative. But all square things have origin in a straight line. Nature creates all beings without erring; this is its straightness. It is calm; this is its squareness. It tolerates all beings equally; this is its greatness. It attains what is right for all without artifice or special intentions. We achieve wisdom when all that we do is as self-evident as what nature does."

I draw the circle of greatness and replace the triangle of vain survival attempts with the square of calmness, as large as will fit, inside this circle. I draw straight lines, corner to opposite corner, to show how triangular powers of human intelligence, emotion, and behavior also have origin in a straight line. I see how this simple picture reveals that every man and woman must live within the circle of nature's greatness; how everyone can and must honor and practice rules of straightness (respect for all life) and rules of calmness (peace); and how individual powers are separate yet one when applied in accordance with rules of greatness, straightness, and calmness.

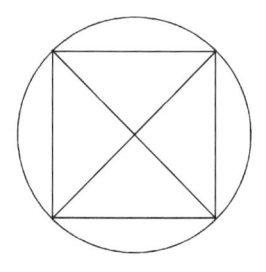

Then I draw another circle that shows the gaps in greatness, from human failures to honor the needs and gifts of all people. I draw the constricted square of failures to honor rules of peace, from vain expectations of relief of distress. Inside this constricted square, I put the crooked lines of corrupted misuse of human power.

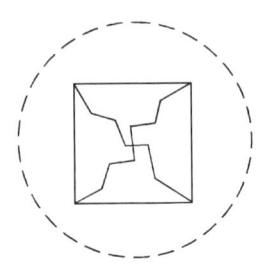

I imagine the straightening of crooked lines of corruption that will happen as more of us admit terrible mistakes and damages—how the lines can be extended to push the corners of the constricted square outward to reconnect with the circle of greatness. I think how vain causes have weakened the walls of the square of calmness and opened them to let in evil, and how constricting the square to conceal breaks in its walls has increased the power of evil, let it in, and prevented its removal.

With the restoration of sight and truth, rulership of goodness is restored. The rest of the work of correcting mistakes will happen naturally. A further conclusion is that we can't yet even imagine the real experience of greatness or calmness. All we can know is what we must do to reconnect with nature.

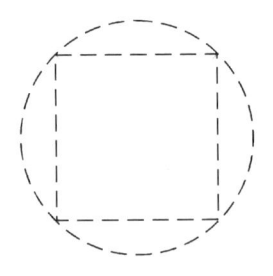

*Chapter 33*

# *Secondary Damages*

All who are in any way dependent on a victim's support in turn become secondary victims. All who suffer mistreatment and their dependents experience serious loss of mental, emotional, and physical well-being, and related loss of abilities of caring.

Because of the tendency to assume victims must have done something they should not have done, thereby causing the mistreatment, even further damage is suffered as a result of wrong judgments. When we most need others' trust and encouragement, even those we're confident will be supportive too often contribute to the suffering.

That my children and I survived the mistreatments we suffered with all faculties essentially intact is truly appreciated, but there seems to be no remedy for the great sadness that we're not nearly as supportive or trusting with each other, or people in general, as we once were. We realize all too well the risks and price of not obliging what all too often turn out to be vain expectations and demands. Even those who sincerely respect my not giving in to threats and abuses tend to attribute this uncommon victory to some special inherent capability, as opposed to simple fervent refusal to cooperate with wrongdoing.

My honesty and sensitivity are more openly criticized also, as though these qualities are more resented than appreciated. Here's where I clearly see the awful power of common though clearly irrational conclusions. Resistance to what we all understand is in everyone's best interest is surely a measure of how fear is allowed to overrule intelligent response to threats to well-being. Nor does it help that bullies and their advocates misjudge those of us who refuse to give in to hurtful pressures to be uncaring. I understand how it may seem we must go along with bullying behaviors, no matter how unreasonable, to avoid even worse mistreatment.

I should clarify that, although I strongly disagree with irrational destructive trends, I'm sympathetic toward all who have neither the desire nor the intention to do harm to anyone yet give passive consent to hurtful practices because it seems to them they must do so to "get along." Somehow we must develop ways and means to not allow dishonest unkind persons to misuse human power and privilege.

## Chapter 34

# *Taurus*

My youngest son was a young boy when he brought home an orange striped kitten that he persuaded me to let move in with us. He named this kitten, born in May, Taurus; the month of May is ruled by the astrology sign Taurus. They were inseparable, except when Taurus took his early-morning stroll through our village's downtown to stop by all the shops as they opened for his morning treats. I don't recall how this daily ritual got started.

This cat also went to my son's school, across from our turnaround driveway, to wait to walk home with him for lunch. They went back to school and came home together when classes ended. This routine became as important in the daily affairs of the shopkeepers downtown, and the kids and teachers at school, as it was to Taurus and my son.

Taurus wasn't a great-looking cat, and some of his habits were borderline disgusting. His favorite resting spot was on top of the back of a green velvet couch with his body wrapped halfway around the neck of the person sitting on it. He purred so loud we poked him to make him stop, but he also drooled copiously whenever he was petted or poked.

Taurus hated the cold and snow. I didn't want litter boxes in the house. We had to keep clean a straw path to his favorite outdoor toilet location. He wouldn't do his toileting if anyone was watching, making long distance travel with him a major challenge.

One day he wasn't on the playground when school let out, and he wasn't at home or anywhere else we thought he might have gone. After weeks of searching and worrying, we agreed something terrible must have happened to him. Then, on a rainy gloomy evening when I was driving home from work, I noticed a dead cat on the side of the road not far from our house. I stopped and got out the car to check if this cat could be Taurus. The same size, gender, orange-striped coat, and scars from fights assured me this was our missing champ. I bundled him in a jacket and took him home. All agreed he had to be Taurus. We made a coffin, had a proper funeral and burial, and laid him to rest, complete with tombstone with engraved eulogy poem.

About a month later, my young son rushed home from school shouting, "Taurus was at school today," insisting "he was trying to get in the window by my desk." We went back to the school, calling and looking all around for our cat. That evening, I almost had my son convinced his wishful imagination was playing tricks when we heard a scratch on the door. We opened the door and in walked Taurus. The reunion was joyous.

But whose missing cat had we buried? To no avail we tried all sorts of ways to find and notify the owner of the dead cat buried in our backyard, including a series of newspaper ads. We had a lot of explaining to do.

Taurus moved with us from that village to our next home in far north country. He didn't favor country life and was forever wandering off, probably looking for shopkeepers and school kids. Then, once again, he failed to return home. By then, my youngest son was attending college, yet he made special trips home, hoping to find his cat.

Months later, Taurus found his way home. But this time, he was in rough shape. Our guess was that he had put up an awful fight with a bobcat that left him without a tail and one ear, and with multiple cuts and puncture wounds. He recovered, however, and stayed close to home for the rest of his life.

*Chapter 35*

# Ducks Unlimited

It's not possible to anticipate springtime without recalling glorious awakenings on the river homestead. Even before the official date, new life burst forth everywhere. One spring, a friend and I hatched ducklings, an impressive mix of exotic breeds—Blue Swedish, Mallard, Indian Runner, Khaki Campbell, Canvas Back. This project began with a dozen fertilized eggs in a small incubator. When they hatched, it was still too cold to put them outdoors. We made a wire pen under the stairs next to the woodstove. They thrived. My dog, Phoebes, true to her sheepdog heritage, stood watch, refusing to leave their side except for occasional breaks to do outdoor rounds.

We built a duck house with a straw floor and surrounding fenced yard. As the ducklings matured, they were allowed to roam the larger pasture. A drainage ditch running through the property was converted into a small pond, with enough overflow to keep the pond water fresh. Phoebes went into the pond with the ducks.

The following winter, we had to provide underfoot protection. We let the ducks in the back woodshed and laid straw over the dirt floor—not one of our better improvisations, we learned, as the multiple layers of straw and droppings thawed. That second spring the ducks started laying eggs and setting. Our flock size more than doubled, with unusual crossbreeding. The babies were swimming in the small pond by the end of that summer. Wild ducks dropped by, at times staying several days.

Needless to say, we had to enlarge the duck house before the following winter and add a straw-covered yard. We realized that overpopulation was a serious problem, especially as hawks discovered this feeding ground. Phoebes was allowed to sleep outdoors to keep watch. We lost two youngsters that winter.

The third spring we lost nearly half the flock. All would seem to be healthy and happy as the day began, but before day's end as many as a half dozen ducks would be dead. Eventually an autopsy showed these deaths were caused by allergic reactions to black-fly bites.

Another huge problem leading to the decision to let go these beautiful birds was the expense and care of keeping them. When I realized I was spending twice as much on food for the ducks as for Phoebes and myself, I knew they were an extravagance I couldn't afford. I put an ad in *The Shopper*, "Exotic Ducks for sale, $2 each." There were no calls. I changed the ad to, "Exotic Ducks need good homes." The phone didn't stop ringing. Two hours after this ad was out, all the ducks were gone. A neighbor complained that I didn't save some for him.

## Chapter 36

# *Chloe*

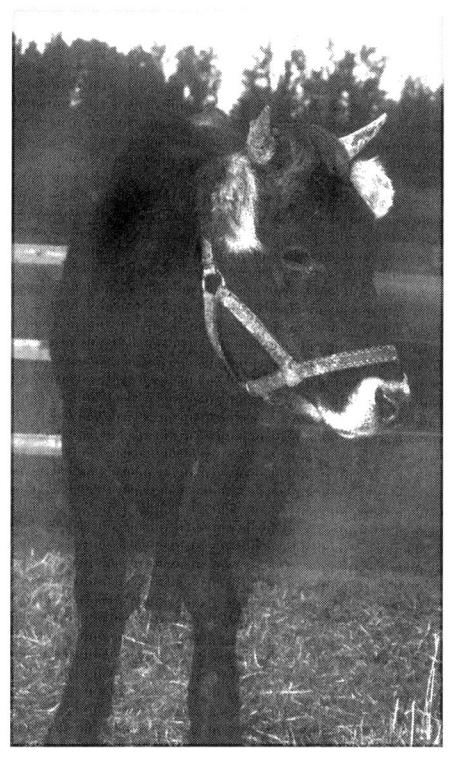

She was a beauty—a young, never-bred "but ready" Brown Swiss cow, complete with horns. The guy across the road from her owner said he had the best bull for mating her. If I left her with this neighbor for a month, the promise was she'd be with calf for sure, giving me time to build her a small barn before cold weather set in.

That homecoming was quite a bit more unsettling than I'd bargained for. No one had mentioned that Chloe jumped five-foot-tall fences with ease. Maybe that explains why she was staked out in an open field? Within ten minutes of unloading, she took off through the woods. A neighbor and I, along with Phoebes, managed to catch up with her. But she wouldn't let us put even a loose rope around her neck to lead her back home, nor could we shoo or coax or corner her.

After dark, we gave up and decided it was up to her. If she wanted to be my cow, she'd find her way back home. Later, as I was getting ready for bed, I heard scraping on the west-side ground-level window—from Chloe rubbing her horns against it. She met me at the fenced field gate, let me give her a hug, and gave Phoebes a kick out of her way as she walked right through.

I was awakened in the middle of the night by frightful cow screams and a thunderous crash. In the moonlight, I could see that the barn framework had fallen down. Chloe had entered this skeleton building through the wide front-door space and tried to exit through the back (where there wasn't a wide enough space), taking the entire structure with her until it collapsed. She suffered no injuries. The barn framework would have to be rebuilt.

That cow was so freaked out that she would never again cross the threshold into that barn. She even went without water and food for days, shivering in minus-forty-degree temperatures, as I was determined all my good work to assure her well-being wouldn't be wasted.

She wasn't "with calf," even after a second full month of lovemaking with the "right bull."

*I think these stories*
*of special relationships with animals, albeit problematic at times,*
*represent better ways of handling differences*
*than persons with opposing strong mindsets tend to use.*

## Chapter 37

# *Abuse of Power and Privilege*

Persons who are employed as professional counselors, teachers, and clergy, but who actually are predators, have long been the focus of concern and speculation. My conclusion is that, to develop ways to effectively prevent this abuse and its far-reaching damages, not to mention the widespread tolerance of such crimes, we must openly share and take seriously all incidents, assigning absolutely no fault or punishment to victims or innocent witnesses. Otherwise, I make no claim to be able to recommend the solution to the victimization of vulnerable persons, except to nip in the bud even what may seem not serious bullying behaviors. I'm confident, as with all destructive acting out, that the underlying error is the mishandling of vital emotions of fear and love.

This story addresses rather common reactions to misuse of professional stature and privilege, how these reactions are often as destructive as the original crimes, contributing greatly to failures of corrective intervention.

I was grateful to receive a job offer with a large religion-based social-services organization. My job was to establish a counseling service in the community and provide counseling. The promise was that this new service would fill the gaps left by other community mental-health resources. There were so many referrals and satisfied clients that it wasn't long before we needed to hire a second therapist.

I employ various helpful aids—including art therapy, storytelling, and role-playing—in the course of counseling, especially when working with children and families. That state's Board of Psychologists (at least at that time) didn't approve of these interventions. When I was told I couldn't be licensed as a psychologist in that state and continue to use these aids, I chose to use my other title, licensed psychiatric nurse. My employer supported this decision, though he explained that we could charge more for my work with a licensed psychologist on staff. It was decided, therefore, that a licensed psychologist would be added at this juncture. I had no objection, of course.

But I was sure from the start that the man hired wasn't the right person. My expressed concerns were dismissed. Within a few weeks, I began receiving complaints about this man's mistreatment of female clients referred to him. He was instructing these women that it was their fault their husbands or male partners were abusive, because they weren't satisfying the sexual needs of these men. He proposed to teach these women how to please their partners sexually.

I passed on these reports to my boss, who said, "I'll take care of it." The reports continued, however. I eventually encouraged those making referrals to take complaints directly to my boss, but there was still no helpful response. So those making referrals simply advised these female clients to seek help elsewhere.

While I was on vacation, one of my female clients was hospitalized, near death, from a beating by her husband. Because I wasn't available, the psychologist recently hired was asked to visit this client. When I returned from vacation, I learned that he had lectured her as to how her husband couldn't stop beating her until she satisfied his sexual needs.

I went to my boss with a request that he report this psychologist's mistreatment of female clients to the proper authorities or I would be obliged to make this report. I was literally ordered to leave my office and not return, with the hostile threat, "If you say anything about this to anyone else, I'll destroy you."

I was devastated. When even church pastors in charge of assuring ethical professional conduct let fear of confronting terrible misuse of professional privilege push them to act to condone horrific mistreatment of vulnerable clients, I find little cause to hope to be able to provide substantial help to victims. Then, when outside professional peers and service agencies in turn admit to being too afraid to support those of us who do stand firm in objecting to such mistreatment, the impact is despair. This experience also reawakened the horror of all church refusals to act responsibly in regard to sexual abuse of children by clergy.

One hospital board member, a lawyer, resigned that position as he encouraged me to take legal action against my employers. But already, there had been so much underhanded manipulative pressure by this powerful church organization for the courts to disregard this action that my attorney was persuaded to withdraw his support. He wouldn't even talk with me about his sudden change of mind. The few witnesses who offered to testify on my behalf, and my clients' behalf, disappeared, literally. When I located one of these witnesses, she admitted being afraid for her life and begged me to never tell anyone where she had gone.

I again retreated to the one place that seemed at all safe. With my dog Phoebes, I hiked up and down the steep riverbank so many times each day and night that we carved a path that other wild creatures began to follow. Sometimes these walks were to ease the unbearable torment that wouldn't let me be still. Sometimes the need came from sheer appreciation of my wild woods and river, not yet corrupted by destructive human habits. Sometimes I was starving for closeness with all that's incapable of senseless violence, as my dog and I settled onto huge rocks at the river's edge, encouraged by the habits of its residents and visitors.

One cold spring day, a flock of geese landed on a floating ice slab. Their show couldn't have been more spectacular if it were staged, as they bathed in the bright sun, enjoying the free ride. Phoebes and I followed this floating show as far along the riverbank as we could, when she swam out to join the geese on one slow turn, giving obvious care to not upset their contentment.

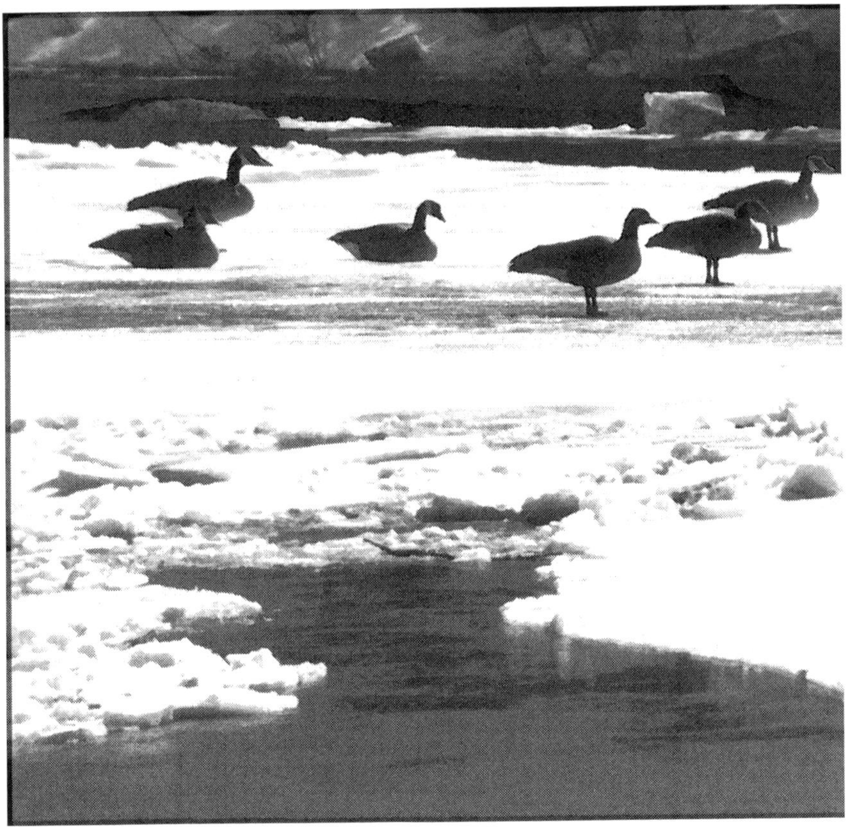

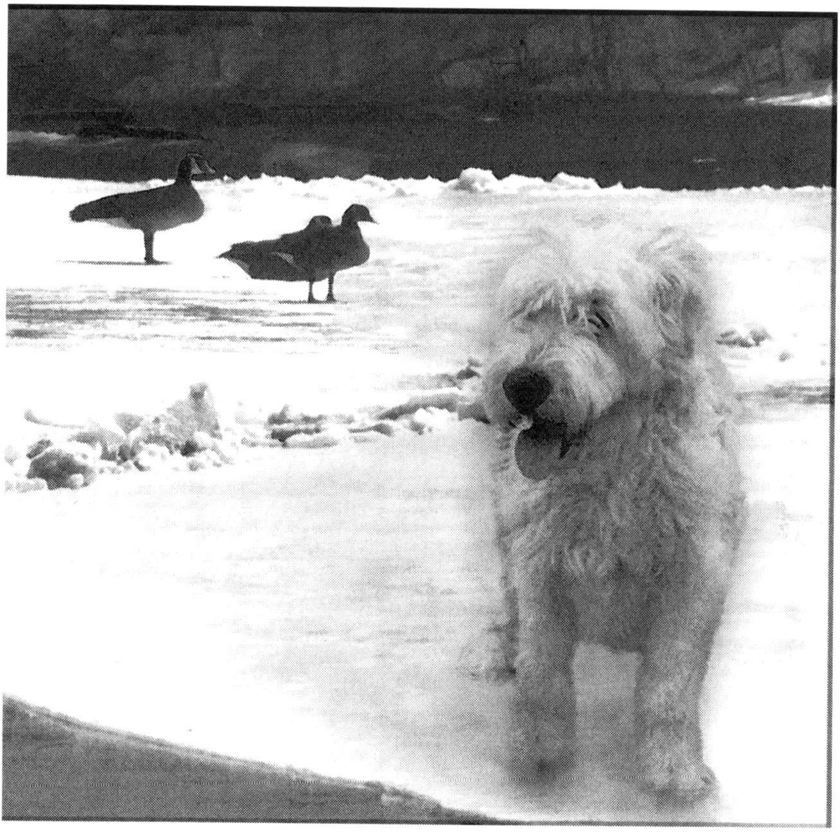

the craving tears deeper inside
every time there's pulling away from
or attack
of vital needs and passions

until I wish I could believe the lie
that fear and love
are the devils
that divide us

until this violence rends my soul
and again I must shout unwelcome truths

*Chapter 38*

# Recovery

There wasn't enough sun and warmth that summer. Neither gardens nor gardeners thrived. The first hard frost came way too soon. Every warm sunny fall day was an occasion to prepare for the hard winter I knew was fast approaching.

The sun porch that I rough-built the previous fall was the ideal place to begin these preparation rituals. As the sun's first rays cast a glow on the river below, I was already waiting with a cup of hot coffee, laying enough fire in the woodstove to protect the porch plants from frostbite. The old well-used and patched rocker creaked back and forth in rhythm with my rushing thoughts as to the best use of what promised to be a glorious day. I stopped rocking and stood on the rocking-chair seat to reach clusters of ripe cherry tomatoes hanging from the porch rafters. As I gently brushed aside the foliage to pick the ripe fruits, I breathed in and held on to the fresh green fragrance.

I was reminded by the woodpile blocking my view of the road that it was time to haul firewood closer to the house, a good job for this cold sunny morning. By afternoon, the ground would be soft enough to start digging and storing beets and carrots—and to bury the dead skunk found in the back shed. That evening, I'd start laying straw on garden beds that needed winter cover.

I moved to the porch table to finish sorting and packing photos from the last family visit so I could take them to the mailbox a short walk up the dirt road. Phoebes waited impatiently by the wheelbarrow. We got seven loads of firewood stacked before we needed a break. By then, the porch was so hot I propped open doors on both sides to let the cool breeze flow through.

The winter that followed was even more difficult than anticipated. After losing my job with the church-sponsored counseling project, I was unable to find another one. The pastor boss who fired me and threatened to destroy me if I talked had notified every mental-health service agency within commuting distance that I'd be looking for a job and that I had been terminated for gross misconduct. I wasn't eligible for unemployment-insurance benefits because I was fired for alleged wrongdoing. I wasn't eligible for other public assistance benefits because my income that year exceeded low-income requirements.

My sole income—from a few private clients, a few loan repayments, and odd photography jobs—averaged two hundred dollars a month. I thought I'd have to abandon my beloved homestead, at least for that winter. But neither friends nor family I asked thought it would work for them to have me stay with them even for a few weeks while I figured out my next move.

I somehow survived the minus-sixty-degree temperatures, my unfinished ill-equipped house, a record snowfall, frozen sewer and water lines, the worst bout of flu ever, car breakdowns I couldn't afford to have repaired, total isolation, and overwhelming unbearable grief.

Once again, I handled unthinkable punishments without human help or caring; once again, I was stripped bare of all doubts as to who I am and who I'm not (as though I had forgotten prior verification). From then on, I've clearly and firmly refused any attempt to pass unreasonable judgment onto my words and actions—unless the person passing judgment has walked in my shoes. (And no one who has walked in my shoes has ever criticized my thoughts or actions.)

I believe the refusal of vain misjudgments may underlie the courage to do the sharing necessary to ending ignorance and arrogance—the precursors of violence.

One of the most difficult and crucial tasks of recovery is letting go of what's in the past—what's done and what's gone, the good and the bad. Every client I've ever helped recover from loss, trauma, and heartbreak has pleaded for me to explain, "How do you just let it all go?"

Eventually I was able to share an image that seemed to help others answer this question. Picture yourself carrying an overwhelming load of attachments and belongings. Some were collected for their pleasure or beauty, some are precious gifts and memories hung onto, some are ugly awful mistakes and abuses inflicted or suffered, some are frivolous hoardings and adventures. Some you're afraid you can't live without.

But you've outgrown all these. You need to make room to take on new life experiences and lessons, and their tools and involvements. So you open your arms and release your grip to let all the pleasurable, the beautiful, the precious, the ugly, the painful, and the frightful stuff of the past crash to the hard floor.

Then you clean up the mess, and you either store whatever is unbroken that may prove useful in the future or pass it on to those in need. You bury or shred or burn or recycle what's broken or otherwise of no good use to anyone. Then you're ready to open your empty arms to welcome, take on, and take care of what's to come.

*So it is that we're constantly challenged to move into and out of nature's extremes, and our own.*

## Chapter 39

# The Price of Integrity

A friend I grew up with recently shared with me his greatest regret. This conversation occurred after the death of a man who was close to both of us, as we were reminiscing about old times. We hadn't been together for years, mostly because his wife objected to our visits.

This friend knew about my losing my job and professional alliances because I wouldn't give in to my boss's threat that if I talked about a colleague's abuse of women clients, "I'll destroy you!" During our talk, he referred to this incident and admitted, "I don't think I'll ever be able to forgive myself for not doing what I knew was the right thing to do, out of fear of losing my job and professional standing."

He shared his story. He was in charge of testing heavy equipment, worldwide, for a giant company he'd been with since graduating from a prestigious engineering school. His relationship with this company was without difficulty until the day his boss directed him to fire one of his employees, a man he described as "more than competent," dedicated, all-around upstanding, and a "best friend."

When he questioned this directive, his boss replied, "I have a guy I want you to give his job to."

"But that's not right," my friend pleaded.

His boss then ordered, "You'll fire him if you want to keep your job, and you'll say nothing about this to anyone else!"

This friend not only fired his employee but also fabricated reasons for this action in an attempt to assign blame to this entirely innocent good man. By the time he finished his confession, he was sobbing. He added that he hadn't acted in accordance with his conscience because his wife insisted he must not do anything to jeopardize his job.

*No matter the price I've paid for not giving in to evil persuasion,
I wouldn't trade places with this friend.*

*Chapter 40*

# The River Boat Trip

One Saturday afternoon, I jumped into my old rowboat with a woman friend who was staying with me at the time, and we headed off for a quick trip to take photos of the riverbank landscape. We left a car at a landing we were sure we'd reach within an hour or so. But we hadn't given due consideration to how many more miles the river travels, with all its backward and forward turns, than the straighter road. We brought no jackets or food; we had only hats, sunglasses, and a camera.

Around the first bend we ran into a neighbor fishing with his young children, who asked where we were headed. We replied, "To the landing ahead."

He remarked, with a doubting look, "Hope you brought tents." We thought he was joking. Around the next bend, we ran into rapids that slammed the boat against huge rocks. Farther along, it started to rain, and soon after it began to get dark. I was grateful I had a weatherproof case for my camera.

We recognized we were in big trouble and started watching for a place to get off the river, hoping to see a house with a path going up the steep bank. We saw no houses and no paths. The bank was far too treacherous to climb, with or without a boat. The sky was without stars or moonlight. We prayed we'd be able to recognize the landing where our car was. We had to get out of the boat every few minutes to lift it over sandy ridges or hand-pull it around boulders and such. We were shaking from the rain and cold and had lost all sense of time and location.

When we thought we saw an opening in the trees—which we hoped marked the landing—we were too exhausted to navigate the rowboat toward it. We left the boat where it got stuck and waded in that direction. It was the right place. We slipped and fell every few steps as we pulled the boat to shore and up the bank. I'm not sure how we managed to get ourselves out of that mess and loaded and back home.

By the time we got home, we were so chilled we soaked in tubs of hot water and drank hot tea to stop the shakes. We wrapped ourselves in blankets and slept as the clock chimed four a.m., sixteen hours after we'd jumped in the boat for a quick river trip. By daylight, we expected we might recover. We ate a hearty breakfast and drove into town for a few groceries and newspapers. We were greeted with, "Morning, ladies. Word is you had a kind of rough adventure last night."

*Not taking due precautions creates dangerous situations, preventable if only honest careful thought is applied in preparing for adventures like quick riverboat trips.*

## Chapter 41

# Helping Children Who Suffer Unthinkable Abuse

Two brothers were abandoned by troubled parents. The older boy, at age three, tried to take care of the infant boy until food and clean diapers were gone. He carried his brother door-to-door asking for help. No help was offered until the second day, when a kind soul called child welfare services. Foster care was arranged, but without regard for the brothers' special bond and need of each other. They were separated and placed in different foster homes.

A childless married couple, both teachers, learned of the plight of these brothers in the course of exploring the possibility of adopting a child. A visit with the older brother ended in their offering to adopt him, with the understanding that needed medical and counseling services would be provided. This boy had become unreachable. The recommendation was long-term intensive psychotherapy.

I was the chosen therapist. This couple even insisted we write a contract stating, as a condition of the adoption, that I would be working with them and this child as needed. Therapy sessions were set at twice weekly. The boy was essentially unresponsive to both verbal and behavioral communication attempts. He scooted into the farthest corner of the room, under a desk, where he assumed a fetal position facing the wall. The adoptive parents and I talked openly about how we might help him become more trusting. For a number of sessions he gave no noticeable response to anything we said or did.

When it seemed time for a more assertive show of caring, I crawled into the corner under the desk with the boy, with a large drawing pad and crayons. As I drew on this pad, I described that I was drawing what I was feeling and thinking about him, how I wanted to help him feel better, how I hoped that he might help me help him by talking or drawing about what he was feeling and thinking.

Eventually he sat up to watch my drawing. After a while, he indicated that a few of my pictures weren't correct. I offered the crayons for him to fix the mistakes. When he complained there was no room on the paper, I asked him to come with me to the much larger drawing pad on an easel stand. He seemed to want to take charge as I suggested we draw a picture of him with his new family. He became totally engrossed in this drawing, wanting no help from me. He was pleased and proud to stand back for a moment to let us enjoy the beautiful family portrait.

Then, using the black crayon, he slowly and completely covered up the drawing. When I asked why he covered his beautiful drawing with the ugly black marks, he replied, "They're my feelings." When I asked if how he felt was like being "afraid" of losing his new family, he let his fears come out in uncontrollable crying.

This was the beginning of a remarkable recovery. The adoptive parents were so pleased they eventually adopted his younger brother. As it was time to enroll the older child at school, the parents were naturally concerned that teasing and bullying by other children would be intolerable. They decided to enroll him in a church-sponsored school, expecting he'd be less apt to be tormented in a religious structured environment.

A few weeks later I received an urgent call, demanding that I come to the school immediately. The new student (my young client) was "out of control," in the boys' bathroom. Though all in charge denied anything had happened to provoke such anguish, as I held and rocked the boy to help him regain composure, I learned from other students that an older student, referred to as "the bully," had pushed and held my young client's head down into the toilet bowl, as he threatened, "You can't get up until you eat your shit."

The older student's action and threat were dismissed as, "That's just kids being kids!" as I was instructed by the school principal that it was my job as a therapist to teach my young client "how to take it."

"Please teach me," I responded. "What is your correct reaction when a bully pushes your head into the toilet bowl until you eat your shit?"

Not long before this incident, due to ongoing complaints about bullying on school playgrounds, I had offered help with this problem. This offer was refused.

Reports of shocking school-related abuses, apparently still thought to be "normal," continued. Another child's head was pounded so hard and so long he was unconscious by the time the bully was finally pulled off him. A report had to be filed with juvenile authorities. In the course of the pounding, the smaller child bit the bully's leg. Both parties were assumed to be at fault, and the child pounded was added to the list of identified juvenile offenders, though the bully wasn't added to this list. The parents who loudly complained were labeled troublemakers.

A child had been assigned to a special-education program, though there were no reports of out-of-control behavior or learning limitations or other disorders. It was discovered that the special-education teacher was sexually molesting this student and others. The child molested was diagnosed as mentally ill and referred to me for care. The special-education teacher wasn't given a label or required to have psychiatric treatment.

A young student subjected to hateful teasing throughout his school experience hated school. As a last resort, his dad taught him how to "beat up" the bullies and instructed him how to not get caught. Teachers commended this student's better attitude, attributing the change to, "We're finally getting through to him."

The student's comment was, "They're all nuts—but they leave me alone now."

It may seem, with all the recent public attention given to bullying, that it's recognized as being unacceptable behavior and therefore simply not allowed. But far too many contrary reports continue for me to believe that intervention efforts are working as intended. There's no acceptable excuse for this failure. When it's clearly understood by all concerned that hurtful behavior isn't allowed, the correct thing to do is to not allow an offender to be with others unsupervised until he or she is able and willing to stop mistreatment without this close attention—until he or she learns to not resort to cruelty in handling insecurities. This is a fairly easy task to accomplish, once it becomes established policy.

I've made innumerable offers to work with teachers and other persons in charge of situations where bullying is an admitted huge ongoing problem. All these offers have been rejected. Why?

## Chapter 42

# *Social-Services Mistakes*

Two bedraggled friendly dogs followed me as I turned off the dirt road onto a deep rutted path to a new client's farmhouse. This family was referred to me as it was recognized that a long series of prior interventions had failed to have intended results. I was instructed to arrange for a police escort to accompany me on home visits because the dad was reported to be hostile toward health-care workers and therefore "dangerous." I didn't follow this advice, fortunately.

Dad answered after several knocks on the side door. He let me enter after I explained who I was and that I had come in the hope of helping his family. He led me through a maze of clutter to the kitchen table that Mom was hastily attempting to clear. As we were all seated, I asked, "So how may I help your family?"

Dad responded, "If you truly care about what help we need, you probably won't have this job long enough to make a difference. We've had do-gooders coming out here for a lot of years and not one has ever asked that question."

I listened as Dad and Mom took turns sharing their story, how Dad was just released from jail for possession of drugs that they didn't know were in their house, how their teenage daughter was taken to a foster home because she was pregnant and Dad was blamed. Dad cried as he gave assurance, "I've not ever had sex with anyone but my wife."

Then this couple continued to share their heart-rending story, how their teenage son was charged with assisting the theft of an AT vehicle, that their younger son was having terrible nightmares and was unable to concentrate on schoolwork, the threats to place both sons in foster care until there was an indoor bathroom.

They described their struggles to survive since Dad lost his job after a back injury, their efforts to build a shop on their property for doing truck repairs for local loggers, how they had no money to finish this project or for a bathroom, that applications for financial help were turned down, that their only income was from selling junk they scavenged at dumpsites.

They explained that they were offered food stamps and fuel assistance, which they don't need because they grow all their own food and have plenty of firewood on their property.

There was a break in our discussion as the two sons arrived home from school. They sat at the table with us to share what help they thought the family needed. Both sons wished for a way to stop hurtful teasing, bullying, and false accusations at school and in the community. They were grateful for their parents' support and each other, and they thought their lifestyle was okay, or would be if they had enough money to finish building their house and truck-repair shop. They left the discussion to do their farm chores and homework.

The parents referred to further abuses suffered—neighbors cutting their fences, letting their livestock out, and then calling police to complain about damages, and on one occasion even setting fire to their unfinished house. They explained how school counselors and police, and even court judges, assumed it was their fault they're tormented because they're "different" from what's considered to be "normal."

We concluded that a good place for me to start helping was with school, police, and court misjudgments, and lack of respect generally. There was a surprisingly good response to this advocacy effort, and even open apologies for past mistakes. I was hopeful we might even be able to enlist a little financial assistance and possibly obtain a grant or loan to help with completion of the house and shop building. Meanwhile, we would work on replacing dysfunctional personal and interpersonal habits within the family that they agreed also handicapped recovery efforts.

Then the program that provided this in-home therapeutic service for at-risk families was cut.

## Chapter 43

# Health-Care Mistreatments

Even as an infant, I suffered unusual sensitivities. Symptoms included skin rashes and hives, digestion problems, persistent cough, and muscle spasms. Baby teeth were subject to decay, requiring extraction and local anesthesia. I became ill after dental procedures, with the sickness attributed to my being overly nervous. I became ill and fainted in church whenever I happened to be seated near someone wearing strong perfume. This sickness was thought to be caused by my not wanting to attend church. (It's true that I didn't want to go to church—because I disliked getting sick.)

Another variance from "normal" was that I was never very sick with ordinary childhood illnesses. The minor symptoms I experienced would have probably gone unnoticed but for careful examination when my brothers developed full-blown cases. (It's not unusual for persons who suffer allergies to be exceptionally resistant to infectious diseases.)

None of my concerns about allergic reactions were given serious attention until I nearly died from a dentist's deliberate mistake. Yet prior to this event, after emergency vein-stripping surgery due to lung blood clots, I had developed a prolonged debilitating illness that was never diagnosed, though I was sure it was caused by multiple local-anesthetic injections. There was even tissue necrosis at injection sites that required skin grafts to heal. Yet doctors insisted my hypothesis was impossible.

Since that awful experience, I've refused all local anesthetics. I suffered through all sorts of dental procedures, from root canals to implants, without any anesthetic. When I developed a sterile abscess, however, the dentist was sure I would need something for pain for him

*Thoughtful Times*

to lance and drain this abscess. I still said, "No!" Then he offered, "I'll inject a little saline [salt water], which will help." But he lied; he injected Novocain. The result was almost immediate cardiac failure.

Since this near-death event, I naturally take extreme care to prevent further lethal errors. As result, most doctors prefer to have nothing to do with me, which they attribute to my being uncooperative. Despite precautions, recently there occurred another serious neglect to honor lifesaving instructions. I was to have an eye exam. Local anesthetic is commonly added to eye drops for dilating pupils. I made a point of asking the assistant to please double-check. She appeared to read the label and said there was no local anesthetic listed, but within minutes after the drops were applied, I began to experience a bad reaction. I yelled to the assistant to get me the allergy medicine in my purse. The eye doctor heard me and came into the examining room. She handed me the bottle of medicine and proceeded to attempt to do the eye exam, though I said, "Please, I can't do that now!"

Both the doctor and her assistant ushered me out the door. My pupils were still dilated. I couldn't see well in the bright daylight. I was drowsy from the allergy medicine, and the allergic reaction had not yet been altogether relieved. I shouldn't have been allowed to leave or operate a vehicle. (One often-overlooked symptom of severe allergic reactions is impaired judgment.)

When I reported this incident to the doctor who made the referral and asked that he support my complaints, he replied, "I can't do that." He referred me to one of the most prestigious medical centers in the world. At this appointment, as I asked to read the label on the eye-drop bottle with an explanation of my concerns, the doctor refused my request. He insisted I'd have to have a thorough allergy workup before he would do the exam.

I had previously applied to have just such a thorough study done and was told, "We can't help you," because my history and symptoms don't conform to established diagnostic criteria and practices. In effect, I'm denied even ordinary health-care services because unusual health problems aren't duly acknowledged in physician training, and because I ask to read medicine labels to insure there are no ingredients I'm allergic to.

For a long time, I believed that needed help with my allergy condition wasn't available because my symptoms were so rare, but by now I've become acquainted with many people with similar sensitivities and can no longer accept that excuse.

As previously mentioned, formaldehyde products cause serious allergic reactions, for me and a rapidly growing number of persons. These products include all sorts of building materials, household cleaners, lotions, and artificial scents. Perfumes are especially lethal and are banned in most health-care facilities. But on the occasion of a recent blood drawing, two women wearing very strong perfume walked into the laboratory. I knew I needed to get out of the lab to find fresh air, but the technician was determined to keep me in the chair until she had my blood. My friend who accompanied me shouted, "She's deathly allergic to perfumes, she needs to get out of here," and saved the day, but I was later told I should be more respectful of the feelings of the women wearing perfume.

## Chapter 44

# Health-Care Angels

I was suffering a gallbladder condition that was determined to be so serious as to require immediate surgery. I was warned by several doctors that, without this surgery, there was a high risk of rupture and death. But these doctors offered no remedy for the problem of my extreme intolerance of local anesthetics and history of life-threatening reactions to some general anesthetics as well. Nor were they willing to investigate possible options outside what seemed a no-win situation.

Though the pain was excruciating at times, I was able to make phone calls between the worst bouts. I called every health-care clinic and hospital within commuting distance. My prayers were answered with the call to the next to last hospital on this list. My call was transferred to the emergency room. A fourth-year medical student answered. He listened to my plight without interruption and then explained, "I'm not able to help you. I'm a student filling in for the nurse who usually answers these calls. But there's a surgeon on call. I'm sure she can help you. I'll have her call you."

This surgeon called within the hour. She asked a few questions to assure she understood my dire situation. She advised, "First off, you need an advocate, someone who knows how to bypass the system's pitfalls. That's me. Then you need to connect with the best surgeon in the country. That's me also. I'll introduce you to the best-in-the-world anesthesiologist. Then we'll need to do a battery of tests to learn everything we can about your physical status. How soon can you get here?"

I was admitted to this hospital the next morning. The surgeon who took charge lived up to all assurances. The anesthesiologist, without the usual harassment of doubting my reports of intolerances, assured me, "We won't give you any local anesthetic. We'll give you a sedative and general anesthetic that you've never had, which will eliminate the possibility of life-threatening allergic reaction. I personally will administer and monitor all medications." (It was his trust in me, I think, that was so reassuring.)

The surgeon introduced me to laboratory and other testing personnel as she explained to them, "You'll answer all this woman's questions and respect her special needs and preferences. If there are any complaints, I'll not be forgiving."

I've never been so well treated. It was decided, eventually, that a couple of other surgical procedures that had been on hold because of anesthesia intolerances could be performed along with the gallbladder surgery. The other surgeons would have to be involved in the preparations, which was accomplished without apparent difficulty. I smoked at the time and had to abstain for a week before the surgery was scheduled. One of these surgeons made the offhand comment, "You should realize by then that you don't need to smoke again after the surgery." I've not smoked a cigarette since.

But there were a couple of glitches in the course of this remarkable feat. On the morning of the scheduled surgery, a different anesthesiologist stopped by my room to introduce himself. He announced, "I'll be administering your anesthesia."

My immediate response was, "No, you're not the anesthesiologist I agreed to let handle this part of the surgery."

It was explained that my assigned anesthesiologist was across town administering anesthesia to another patient. He had mistakenly written my scheduled surgery on his calendar for the next day. "We'll wait," I said.

"We can't do that," was the reply. When the "guardian angel" surgeon learned of this mistake, she immediately arranged to have the available anesthesiologist relieve my guy across town so that he could fulfill his obligation to me.

*Thoughtful Times*

All was in order as promised, and the technician was about to start the pre-op IV and wipe the skin area with the customary alcohol sponge. Fortunately, I was still alert enough to yell, "Is there local anesthetic in that sponge?" The technician then remembered the warnings posted everywhere that I'm deathly allergic to local anesthetics.

I'm very sure few hospital patients receive the special treatment and accommodations described in this account—a forever appreciated lifesaving experience. Yet there were mistakes that too easily could have had life-threatening impact.

It seems the underlying failure is that health-care systems and most institutions aren't set up to give due regard to human differences.

*Chapter 45*

# *Reflections*

I think a lot about what I could or should have done differently in the awful interactions described in some of the stories shared in this book. As I play out in my mind various possibilities, I realize there's surely cause and room for improvement in my handling of terrible abuses. But is there a right and wrong way to handle mistreatment? It seems to me the errors belong primarily to the persons who commit the hurtful actions, whether accidental or intentional.

We who suffer mistreatment, however, have a responsibility to require, encourage, and assist correction of mistakes without resorting to "hurting back." At times I even question if I should assume a strictly defensive position from the start, yet I'm fairly alert, I believe, to others' careless tendencies and sincerely believe my policy of trusting until there's good reason to not trust is best.

I wonder if it's even possible to assure we'll be treated with due regard when persons in charge of so many important life transactions all too often haven't earned that honor and privilege. When this is the situation, the outcome of disagreements, large and small, is commonly determined by devious avoidance and manipulations of rules and policies, as opposed to what's correct and fair.

Many of my experiences of mistreatment erupted when I accidentally ran into others' transgressions, and wrongdoers were afraid I'd make complaints that put them at risk. They took action against me to assure I wouldn't dare reveal my accidental discoveries of their wrongdoing. It's doubtful that these persons will willingly adopt better ways of handling fears.

My thoughts are apt to take a different direction as it occurs to me that "fight-or-flight" instincts, when allowed to take charge of how fear is handled, seem to work better in the animal kingdom than for humans. Possibly it's our gift of so-called higher intelligence that best explains this variance. As with all special gifts, higher intelligence comes hand-in-hand with greater responsibility. When we don't apply intelligence in figuring out ways to act on fear that take into account everyone's need to feel safe and well used, we invariably make worse the threatening situation that is the cause of our fear.

There's a deep sadness that doesn't allow me to become overly hopeful that enough people will commit to the simple common-sense changes I envision, to make a remarkable difference. Perhaps I should simply be grateful that I've personally fared as well as I have. Although my lifestyle resembles that of a hermit, there are enough creatures and people in my life to give joy and purpose, as though we were bound to meet, whatever our circumstances. It's not that I believe all that happens is part of a large life scheme or plan, but rather that we attract and find each other as we're ready to give and receive as wanted and needed.

Maybe we have to suffer abuse personally, even, to understand why and how it must be stopped? But all of us do suffer in some ways the hurtful impact of all mistreatment. Until everyone's needs and abilities are well attended, no one can achieve his or her true and full potential.

*Mary Lax*

Again, sad heavy thoughts take me back to knowing that we're all on one and the same huge life vessel. Our likenesses and differences have connective threads waiting/begging to be drawn and pieced together, for us to have the understanding needed to make it possible for each and all of us to be safe and free.

## Chapter 46

## *Assuring Truth in Sharing*

I'm thinking about attempts to restrict sharing and how such attempts seem to have their origin in fear of losing control of what and how information is exchanged, as though being in control of information exchange is assumed to be essential to well-being. It's my experience that this is an erroneous assumption. The need is to take care to assure information acquired and passed on is true and relevant and that there's no agenda other than learning and teaching. With these simple precautions, it's my belief that open and free sharing of information cannot be harmful.

I also realize that, to be truly useful, the gathering and dispersing of information requires careful management, which means taking care to not omit information necessary to understanding or to include data that's unsubstantiated, in the process of acquiring and passing on experience and knowledge. Such precaution is especially difficult because we're well trained to "fill in the blanks" with unwarranted assumptions.

Medical science, for instance, has a starting place—the disease, its symptoms, and its cause. The ending place is treatment and cure. This seems to work well so long as cause and cure are identifiable. But when cause and cure aren't obvious, treatment is confined to symptoms, and there's much guessing. Although this guessing may follow scientific rules, it easily takes a wrong turn. New symptoms may be masked by the treatment and overlooked. Treatment might also alter healthy functions. It's not possible to keep track of all variables. The focus of study must be narrowed to keep research manageable, which carries a risk of limiting consideration of possible causes and cures.

There's another way to keep research manageable, and that's by working within the structure of the life circle—the seed, the seedling, the plant, the flower, the fruit, and back to the seed. We know that, if this circle is broken, life ends. We know that less serious disruptions can be repaired and functions restored. If there's careful observation to determine where, how, and when disruption occurs, the study naturally takes on focus that has the best chance of leading to corrective intervention.

Again, let's consider the affective disorder referred to as "depression." We know the symptoms—feelings of helplessness and hopelessness, eating and sleep disturbances, difficulty performing mental and physical tasks that are ordinarily easy, obsessive concern with real and imagined threats to well-being, suicidal ideation that may precipitate suicide attempts, etc. We don't know the cause, although there is much expert speculation (and disagreement). There are many different views as to the best intervention, from antidepressant drugs to directives to "shape up"—or even, when more conservative treatments don't have the desired outcome, confinement in a psychiatric institution. Symptoms may be relieved by one or another intervention, or they may be aggravated. New, even worse symptoms may develop. Or, despite intervention, suicide or insanity can be the tragic outcome.

It's my belief that we can and should do less guessing and rely more on readily accessible information. I ask lots of questions to gain better understanding of what needs and abilities aren't being well monitored and attended, what's not working in attempts at well-being and satisfaction, and what promises to be the best way to begin to correct the failures. I also thoroughly explore the seldom-asked question, "What are the kept secrets?"

I reflect all this information back to the client with the aid of simple references and drawings and encourage him or her to begin to make changes in living habits in accordance with this knowledge, with reassurance that I'll be available to lend needed support. Except where there is persistent strong resistance to making needed changes in unhealthy life habits, invariably the problem of depression is solved.

When resistance to change prevents recovery, full attention must be given to whatever powerful fears underlie resistance and to developing ways and means to relieve their power and to reaffirm how needed changes won't have hurtful outcome.

It's necessary to face head-on the terrible truth that our inclination to assume that what is familiar is safer than what is unfamiliar is a huge handicap. Though it's natural to be a bit apprehensive whenever we explore the unknown, this apprehension is intended to help us proceed with caution. With practice, we soon develop confidence that relieves apprehension, and at that point making beneficial changes becomes an exciting challenge.

There's a real difference in feelings of fear that warn of actual danger and feelings of apprehension that accompany unfamiliar experiences. They're not difficult to distinguish when this is the conscious intention.

## Chapter 47

# *An Artist Friend*

We met accidentally. Her brother was a neighbor of mine, and she belonged to an artist's guild where she became friends with another neighbor. I liked her paintings, which she proudly displayed and described. Her painting style was mostly impressionist. Her talent and skill were obvious, but even more appealing was the striking revelation in these paintings of this woman's deepest and highest moods and insights.

She showed up without notice one evening at my back door with a suitcase. As I invited her inside, she explained she had learned I was developing a new method of reproducing original paintings as fine-art prints and decided I should do this work for her. She opened her suitcase filled with assorted boxes of photo slides, with further announcement that these were the paintings she thought "we" should start with. She explained she had made these photos of her early paintings as they were sold, admitting, "They're not the best quality."

I was being polite as I held several slides she handed me to the light for quick appraisal. As she continued to describe her expectations about sharing her paintings with the world, I felt an urgency to make her aware that these slides were of such poor quality and so damaged they wouldn't reproduce well, but she gave no serious attention to my discouraging speech as she continued to sort through the slides.

I had never dealt with a person this openly determined to have me do what she wanted. I listened and waited for an opportunity to interject information I needed her to accept. As she continued to share her feelings and thoughts nonstop, along with her entire life history, I realized that this woman didn't give in to handicaps. Eventually I began to wonder if taking on this challenge might even help me achieve my ambitions. I offered to scan a few of the slides to view the images on the computer monitor. With each appearance of damaged and missing parts of the photo slide image, she referred to remedies she was sure I could apply with Photoshop tools.

Her story was an up-front report of extreme neglect, severe hardship, and brutal mistreatment. She admitted there was irreparable damage "to my heart, my mind, my body." But she made sure I understood that she wouldn't have become a great artist if she hadn't suffered such hurt, that her art was her means of connecting with all other survivors, "and these are the people I need and love most."

After months of intense work together, we did end up with a collection of impressive fine-art prints. Fellow artists wanted prints made of their paintings. This was the beginning of my fine-art repro business, still thriving after over twenty years.

This great friend died several years ago after a courageous battle with breast cancer and multiple strokes. Before she died, she reminded me in all sorts of ways of the importance of our relationship. She was sure we were kindred souls destined to find each other.

She gave permission for me to share prints of her paintings with my family and close friends as special gifts. She made paintings "just for you" in appreciation of my help, not only with artistic goals but also with numerous special needs, including driving her wherever she needed to go after she lost her driver's license. She never made apologies for needing and requesting this help, which I appreciated.

She presented one of these paintings as, "Your portrait!" The view was from behind as I stood overlooking the great river where I lived at the time. I teased her with comments like, "I bet mine is the only portrait ever done of one's backside."

She laughed as she replied, "I gave up trying to do justice to your front side."

This painting became the logo for my fine-art printing business, and it's the cover image for this book.

As I wrote this story, I more fully realized how this relationship became as important as it was to both of us—in large part because this exceptional woman was so up-front with her intentions and expectations. Guessing was never necessary, whereas with too many folks, I'm never sure what's expected of me, though I'm made aware of displeasure as I fail to do what's expected.

## Chapter 48

# *Growth in Progress*

It's not easy to admit that some damages from neglect and abuse are irreparable. Even as we recover our ability to care and make room for new experiences, and as we find that our mind, heart, and soul still seem mostly intact, these essential parts that have been spared "death" aren't as strong or obliging as they once were. They'll probably always need special protective care.

For a long time, I was reluctant to share my worst life experiences because of my fear of further hurtful reaction. Only as my need to write this book became more tormenting than the fear of further mistreatment, and I took on this project, did I recognize that I'm not writing this book out of love or fear. It's not a personal thing at all. It comes from a deep sense that it's unfinished work that I still have to do—that I have an obligation to share what I've learned about abuse and recovery. This knowledge must be freely exchanged in order for us to make and follow a more effective course for ending violence.

I now realize how writing about experiences requires a different perspective than living them. We have to rewind the sequence of events and circumstances in slow motion to reexamine them in a brighter light and larger scope than is possible as all this is happening. In the telling, all the parts become more clearly connected. We even become more appreciative that we can create new methods and paths of protection and recovery, a rather commendable achievement in itself. There evolves a

*Mary Lax*

much greater, more solid regard for all human sensitivities and abilities, leaving us far more confident that what we all need most in the way of better treatment is the stopping of all punishment, especially for doing what we know is the right thing for us to do.

## Chapter 49

# Aunt Esther

She was the eldest of eight children and grew up with various family businesses—grocery, real estate, newspaper, retail. At age thirteen, she was hired as a clerk in an uptown clothing store. "She has the knack," explained the store owners, who gradually added to her responsibilities and privileges. She learned purchasing, accounting, marketing, and store management.

When she was sixteen years old, she wanted to visit California. Her employer had a brother in the clothing business in San Francisco who welcomed her talents. She learned clothing design, high fashion, and modeling, and she fell in love with this beautiful city. She saved most of the money she earned and learned to invest this money wisely. When she was eighteen years old, she contracted to buy her own store, with the help and full support of former employers.

She was physically gorgeous as well as smart and ambitious. She had many suitors, until she found the "love of my life," a prominent senator. But because she realized she couldn't be a good wife and mother and have the career she wanted, she refused his proposal of marriage.

The store she bought was so successful she bought a second store. She hired another smart ambitious woman to manage the new store. They eventually became business partners and close friends, and even shared a home. Aunt Esther must have recognized my own adventurous inclinations and my need to not be held back by what was assumed to be a woman's role. She shared regrets that she didn't marry the man she loved, "but now," she stressed, "women can have family and career!"

She was so pleased when I announced my engagement that she flew cross-country to meet my husband-to-be. The three of us had a marvelous time. She had to return to San Francisco the next day, but she promised to send plane tickets for us to visit her after we were married. She also sent a generous check as a wedding present.

We learned she was in the hospital for emergency surgery. Two days later, we received notice that she had died unexpectedly of a pulmonary embolism. My father cashed the wedding-present check for us. Although he gave us the money he kept the check itself. It was the last check she wrote.

Nearly sixty years later, when sorting through saved memorabilia during the move to my current home, I uncovered a yuletide letter Aunt Esther sent friends and family a few years before she died. As I reread this letter, I realized we shared much more in the way of similar life appreciation and attitudes than adventurous inclinations that were prone to being misjudged as wild and foolish. We shared as well the deep and lasting appreciation of uncommon friendships that lend the kind of support and assistance that sustain us along the way of unusual and difficult life journeys.

My thoughts moved ahead to my wanting to share with the world this special yuletide letter and finally let out of the piles of kept treasures, along with its great love and its wishes so honestly, lovingly, and beautifully expressed.

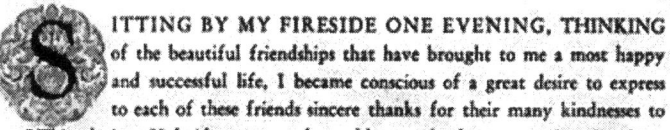

**S**ITTING BY MY FIRESIDE ONE EVENING, THINKING of the beautiful friendships that have brought to me a most happy and successful life, I became conscious of a great desire to express to each of these friends sincere thanks for their many kindnesses to me. ¶ This glorious Yuletide season and an old scrap book gave me inspiration. Accordingly, I pass on to you, slightly altered, a Christmas and New Year's wish, which I beg of you to accept as my heartfelt wish for this lovely season and the year to come.

"The sun is just rising on the morning of another day, a Christmas day heralding a Happy New Year. What can I wish that this day, this year, may bring to you? Nothing that shall make the world or others poorer, nothing at the expense of other men; but just those few things which in their coming do not stop with you, but touch you rather, as they pass and gather strength:

"A few friends who understand you and yet remain your friends.

"A work to do which has real value without which the world would feel the poorer.

"A mind unafraid to travel, even though the trail be not blazed...An understanding heart... A sight of the eternal hills and unresting sea, and of something beautiful the hand of man has made... A sense of humour and the power to laugh.

"A little leisure with nothing to do.

"Tolerance toward your fellow man.

"A few moments of quiet, silent meditation. The sense of the presence of God...And the patience to wait for the coming of these things, with the wisdom to know them when they come."

The wish of one who appreciates your friendship and hopes to sincerely merit this friendship always. ¶ Again expressing to you and yours the season's most inspirational and beautiful thoughts, may I sign myself.

*Long Esther.*

## Chapter 50

# Betrayal

I had recently decided to let go a home and life style I had built and enjoyed for twenty-plus years. I was no longer able to take care of this homestead alone or find needed caretaking help. I met a man who lived near a large community of artists, offering potentials for enlarging my art-repro business. He introduced me to resident artists he met through his serving on the board of the art council. As I became confident this was a right move, he suggested I might move in with him, though he seemed relieved when I decided I should have my own house in town. From the start, he spent a lot of time with me at this town house, and gradually we assumed a kind of life partner status.

We each have a few handicaps and related peculiar habits that at times require special accommodation. As already explained, my most difficult-to-live-with problem is my extreme sensitivity to a number of products, everything from common household materials to body lotions and ointments. This man seemed willing to take care to not bring such into my house—with numerous life-threatening mistakes, however.

My townhouse itself turned out to be a major threat to health, though I was able to improve the situation considerably with various upgrades of the heating and cooling systems. Even when I was fairly sure this man was using products known to make me sick, I hesitated to lay blame because there were so many other possible culprits.

When I built my toxin-free house in the country I looked forward to being able to live without huge doses of antihistamines and the dreaded emergency-room episodes. This man was supportive and accommodating throughout the search for the right property and the planning and building of this new home. Immensely appreciative, I took care to assure his special needs and preferences were given due account, as I wanted him to feel welcome in this new place.

For several months after moving in I enjoyed remarkable health benefits, but then I started having the terrible reactions again. This man assured me he wasn't using any troublesome products, but as the terrible reactions got worse, he admitted he was using these products again. When I became upset with him he gathered a few of his belongings and walked out.

Weeks passed before he stopped by briefly, allegedly to burn a pile of brush. He didn't announce his arrival or ask if burning brush was okay. I was recovering from fractured ribs and a bruised body from a bad fall on the ice. I had to drag myself outside to interrupt this activity.

He asked if he could come out to watch the Super Bowl. I explained that this wouldn't work for me—that first we should talk about what happened and how to prevent further mishaps. Later he stopped by again to bring several grocery items. He asked if I needed anything else. I admitted to needing help still with grocery shopping. He agreed, and we set a date. He did one further shopping trip but again refused my invitation to talk about what happened in effort to "make things right." Weeks later, he came to pick up the rest of his belongings. I haven't seen or heard from him since. This was over three years ago.

I can't help wondering if this man was ever concerned about my well-being, or if he just pretends to care to get what he wants from others and then, when there's objection to his devious ways, he abandons the relationship.

If there was real caring, I think he'd at least say, "I'm sorry!" If he had simply reached his limits of tolerance of my unusual sensitivities, the decent way to handle this would have been to admit up front his unwillingness or inability to make the necessary compromises to share my home. We could even have continued our friendship, just not in my house so long as he must use the lotions and ointments that make me sick.

*Those who don't admit their fears are most likely to cause harm.*

## Chapter 51

# *Second Thoughts*

Though I thought at the time I wrote the preceding story that I had done all that I could to help this relationship work well for both of us or end without irreparable harm to either, I was still tormented by a sense that mistakes could and should have been easily corrected. I realized this story wasn't finished, which made it impossible to finish this book. I wrote the following letter to this friend:

> Hi _____,
>
> It promises to be a beautiful day here. I'm wishing I could spend it outdoors, but I'm committed to putting the finishing touches on the book I'm writing. This book is about relationships—those essential to well-being, those that turn out to be hurtful, what decides the different outcomes, how to fix mistakes.
>
> There's, of course, the story of our relationship, the story that I can't yet give right closure. I went to sleep last night with a request: "Please may I dream about how to finish this story?" In this dream you and I were traveling together, visiting old friends, making new friends. We were much more attentive to each other's needs, limitations, and ambitions in this dream than I recall we actually were. We more openly shared our thoughts and feelings, especially in regard to our fears and vulnerabilities—and we held hands a lot. There

was a sense of greater trust in the dream, the kind that comes from openly talking about respective likenesses and differences.

When I awoke from this dream, I knew what to do to finish this story. The need is to share this dream with you and ask if you might by chance like for us to fix our mistakes. Whatever your response is to this request will determine the ending of this story and its place in my book.

Please know our relationship was and is important and special to me. I've always wanted us to talk more openly about our needs and interests. I've tried to be upfront with you, but it has seemed to me that you prefer "distance." I can't stop thoughts that it would make my day if you would say to me, sincerely, "Hey, I'd like to read your book."

I'll add this letter to you to the story about our relationship written thus far. I'll wait a few days for a response, which I'll add to this story as well. Or, if there is no response, I'll end the story with acknowledgment that there's no reply to this letter.

Mary

There was a reply to my letter. He didn't address its questions, however. He instead referred to how rebuffed he felt when he came to burn the brush pile and I intervened, when I refused his request to come watch the Super Bowl, and because I didn't want him running my dog by way of driving his car ahead, fast. So he just gave up.

I responded, stating that I appreciated his reply and that it seemed he cared, again with request that we talk about our respective needs that weren't well attended. I mentioned that I was still hopeful we could remedy our failures, should he want to make these repairs—again with reassurance that this was my hope.

There's been no further response.

## Chapter 52

# The Generator Project

I was planning and saving to install a propane backup generator for my all-electric power system in my current home. As I accumulated needed funds, I expected it would be a simple matter of hiring a generator expert to assess needs and recommend the appropriate equipment and installation. We'd write a purchase and service contract, and the job would get done.

Sadly, I learned that's not the way it works. I hired a company to do the needs assessment and make recommendations, after which I did a little further study of various options with the conclusion that what was recommended was the best choice. Then I learned that this company provided equipment only; I would have to employ an electrician to install it and a propane company to hook up the gas.

By the time I found an electrician willing to take on this project after three others said they were booked up for months and one other gave me a cost estimate but didn't follow through, the equipment purchase offer had expired. That company also no longer sold the recommended generator. The generator recommended at this time would be more expensive and couldn't be delivered for several months.

Meanwhile, a customer aware of my difficulties brought with him an electrician who offered to do "the whole job" at comparable cost and guaranteed the job would be up and running by the coming April, but he needed an up-front payment. I agreed. April came and went, with no further word or action. In late May, the concrete pad was laid for the generator. Months later, the generator itself was delivered. Over a month after this delivery, the electrical hookup was done—after several reminders as to the long-past date I was assured this project would be finished.

Despite promises that the propane hookup would follow within the week, again there was no further word or action. During this wait, there was a prolonged power outage. I wrote a letter, rather firmly yet respectfully describing the hurtful impact of the failure to honor our signed contract. Within three days, I received an apologetic response and the gas was hooked up promptly. When I made the final payment, my check was returned with further apology for not honoring our agreement as promised.

I truly appreciate this electrician's effort to make things right, a rare and encouraging response to a rightful complaint, but I'm still waiting for the promised lesson on operation and maintenance of this generator system.

*And it would make so much better sense for all involved to simply honor such agreements.*

## Chapter 53

# *Idle Thoughts*

My view of humanness opened up as I allowed thoughts to freely come and go during a break from serious work. I realized a primary focus has been on defensive reactions that represent fear of human differences. I'm also aware of the reluctance to admit our likenesses, how vain efforts to become stronger, richer, smarter, better-looking, and sexier than our fellow humans—expecting that then we'll be less subject to misfortune and mistreatment—make us more vulnerable and therefore more fearful.

It may prove necessary to admit our likenesses to recognize how our differences let us do together what we can but wish to be able to do alone—to insure everyone's needs and talents are well attended and thereby establish peace and good will.

We need to explore such speculations together to better understand the role fear assumes in our interactions. As it is, most of us look to designated experts for the answers. This approach is strongly recommended, and even required, in higher-education pursuits. For example, I intended that my master's degree thesis would show how exploring outside and beyond what's already established knowledge and practice is important to solving horrible human problems. At first, this proposal was approved. Later I was told I must include in my thesis the theories and methods of recognized authorities. I ended up using data from explorations outside set boundaries to show where and how established theories and methods fail. Not only was I criticized for questioning what's considered dogma, but also this report became a focal point of fighting among university staff.

> *All things are known by their differences from*
> *and likenesses to each other.*

## Chapter 54

# *Worse Than Unbearable*

When I made the move from the place of intolerable senseless attacks to the river place of recovery, I met a remarkable woman, a neighbor. Our relationship grew from helping each other with problems once in a while to "best friends." Piece by piece, we shared our experiences of not giving in to cruelty, determined to build a good life.

This friend was sexually molested as a child, with no one to turn to for help. Her subsequent withdrawal and shyness were diagnosed as mental retardation by school counselors. Her physical health problems were attributed to mental problems, also, though years later it was determined she was born with a colon anomaly that caused obstructive spasms. Her early marriage ended in divorce as result of the couple's inability to be loving and supportive in relationship with each other after their infant daughter's death from SIDS. Before their breakup, they were encouraged to adopt an infant daughter. The adopted daughter was bitten by a poisonous spider and nearly died as well.

Eventually, both parents were able to reclaim a friendly relationship and even enjoy sharing parenting of their adopted daughter. They both found new life partners. My friend's second marriage seemed the perfect match. She and her new husband were devoted to each other. They developed a dedication to totem-pole carving that turned into a business earning worldwide acclaim. Their interpersonal and worldly success was indeed commendable.

Last winter, this remarkable woman was killed. The report was that a fifty-foot-tall totem pole she and her husband were carving accidentally fell on her. Though this seemed impossible, given the fact that it was secured in a cradle set low to the ground, no one questioned the truth of the accident report.

Later, however, it was rumored that her husband was having an affair and pressuring her to agree to a divorce, that they were fighting the day of the accident. It was also noted that her husband's story was remarkably different on various occasions of questioning. Eventually there were murder charges against him.

Then a sister of the woman killed reported that it seemed unlikely there was an affair or intentions of divorce, that these stories were maliciously "made up." But just as the trial for murder was about to begin, this man confessed that his hateful aggressive reactions to his wife's refusal to consent to a divorce caused the "accident," and even that his intent was to kill his wife. In the final guilty plea, he also admitted failure to try to help her as she lay dying under the totem pole that crushed her.

Because of this guilty plea, which precluded trial for murder, the maximum sentence was thirteen years, with the possibility of parole much earlier.

## Chapter 55

# Fear Handled Fairly Well

This story describes a recent test of my ability to handle my fears. Ordinarily I'm fairly cautious when interacting with animals, especially creatures in the wild, though not overtly fearful. I've lived in wilderness country most of my adult life. I've shared my country homes with trusted well-trained dogs that have greatly helped me handle potentially dangerous wild-animal situations.

My dogs and I usually manage to teach animal intruders that we're glad to share our space on earth with them so long as they don't make it too difficult for us to take care of our life needs and affairs. When this regard isn't forthcoming, I employ help as needed to move animal trespassers to locations where there's less human activity.

I've lived in my current country home for about four years. Animal creatures stop here regularly to devour edibles in my gardens and woods, to use my driveway as a path from the dirt road behind my house to the

*Thoughtful Times*

river in front, and to just hang out. Squirrels and big birds and such even peck access holes in outside storage cans and wait and watch patiently, expecting to find ways to come inside my house and garage. But there's never been any serious threat to my well-being.

Early one morning, my current dog buddy became more upset than I'd ever witnessed. He was barking frantically, moving from window to window. Annoyed that he awakened me so early, I got out of bed to let him outside to take care of whatever was upsetting him. But at the side deck door a black bear on hind legs was peering at us through the upper glass pane. This bear wouldn't move away from the door, no matter how long and loud we barked or shouted, banged on pots, and blew whistles. I noticed this bear had already destroyed some bird feeders after bending down quarter-inch rod hangers to get to them.

I went downstairs to the studio door to walk out and around the house to where the bear was parked, equipped with a broom and a weed-whacker to chase him away, but the bear was determined to stay put on the deck. My dog hugged my legs, still barking though unwilling to make a further aggressive move.

Eventually I went back around the house to answer the phone. As I described the situation to my son on the phone we agreed that black bears don't usually attempt to enter occupied homes, that something wasn't right with this bear and that I should call for help.

I called a parks-service expert who explained that I shouldn't worry; the bear would leave when he had finished eating all the spilled bird food. But the bear didn't leave. He continued to block the doorway, shifting his position occasionally to peer through nearby windows. When he took brief leave to explore beyond the deck, I snuck outside to water a few plants and clean up the mess of the broken feeders, feeling a bit at risk.

As day turned to night and I couldn't see what the bear was doing, I was even more uneasy. I was actually plain *scared* as I heard him rooting around trying to open outdoor storage containers and doors. I called a friend in town trained to handle such emergencies, and she drove out with her neighbor. Both brought guns and offered to show me how to use them and to leave them with me, not to shoot the bear but to scare him away. By the time they arrived, the bear was no longer on or near the deck, nor did he return while they were around. We agreed all was probably safe, at least for the night.

I wondered why this particular bear provoked such strong fear. I've had bears hang out at other country homes with little cause for concern. But I've learned I should trust my instincts, which told me I wasn't overreacting. My fear wasn't that I personally was in great danger, but that the bear could so easily break a glass door or window, get into my house, and destroy its interior. This bear surely acted as though he intended to get inside.

At one point, when he was on his hind legs staring at me from the other side of the window, paws pressed firmly on the glass, I stared right back at him and shouted, "You may not come into my house!" Maybe he got the message? I've taken similar assertive stands with humans who seem inclined to destroy what I've built, and it usually interrupts such intentions.

The next day, the bear didn't come close to the house, but my dog knew he was still in the woods nearby. He was back on the deck the following morning, but eventually left without further threatening behavior.

## Chapter 56

# *Closing Comments*

I make no claim to have all the answers needed to end violence. My claim is that I know and practice, and work to share, foolproof simple rules for making huge improvements in how we interact with each other—and that, until at least this shift is made, it's unreasonable to expect remarkable improvements in personal or global affairs.

I'm also confident that, as we more openly share the stories of our failures and successes in handling basic life responsibilities, we'll develop even greater understanding of the ways and means, and the importance, of assuring that everyone's needs and capabilities are given due consideration in all interactions and humane causes.

I believe my stories give substance to my claim that truthfulness and kindness assure safe, satisfying relationships for all participants. Stories that depict the craziness of pretending all is well, ignoring or denying unthinkable crimes and far-reaching damages, verify absurdities and undue risks of such self-protective attempts, and harm done when truthfulness and kindness are not given priority consideration.

Though I'm still hopeful this book will encourage and assist crucial changes, I'm also plagued with doubt-filled questions. Is there real cause to even try to persuade people to stand strong together in, for example, refusing to patronize companies that knowingly put life-threatening substances into their products and market them as safe and even beneficial to health? And what can be more destructive to all life than companies polluting air, earth, and waters with toxic wastes that we all know kill—then spending millions of dollars in attempt to wrongly convince us these crimes are safe practice and necessary to economic survival?

Then I must wonder "why" don't we stand strong together, refusing to allow this destruction? How do we manage to justify letting individuals and institutions pledged to serve human needs—including health-care professionals, schools, churches, courts, businesses—ignore or deny or excuse horrific abuses of those they're hired and committed to serve? Why are we not so appalled as we learn that those in charge keep secret these crimes to protect abusers and themselves, instead of attending to at least basic responsibilities to victims, that we must shout, "NO?" And how does anyone justify punishing the few who do refuse to placate demands and actions of offenders and their protectors?

All such blatant failures to take seriously responsibilities that belong inherently to every adult person serve as proof that we are, in fact, giving in and giving way to evil rulership of our lives and our world. All violations of basic human and environmental needs and responsibilities—all failures to honor rules of truthfulness and kindness—contribute to this burden of guilt. There is no truly valid reason for not refusing to be a participant (whether active or passive) in any claim or action that's in any way dishonest or uncaring.

*We have to live with ourselves and each other, and so we ought to be fit for ourselves and each other to know.*

## **End**

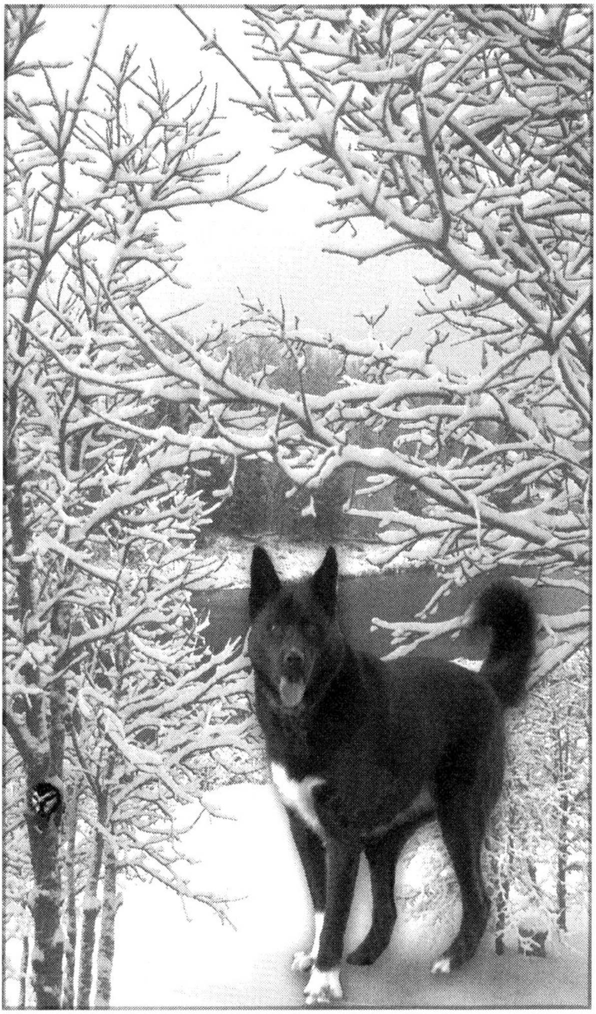

# *Postscript*

A major handicap has plagued me throughout the writing of this book. As I've offered to share this project with close family and friends—and a few other folks I thought would be interested—only a couple of these persons have provided needed feedback. I'm still unable to make sense of this lack of response, as none of these persons will yet even share with me their reasons for refusing this request.

A book publisher who also happens to be a customer did review my writing, however, and said she liked the stories—and that these are "the strength of the book." She wasn't impressed with the discussion chapters. Then an editor I was referred to said she thought the stories were irrelevant, and that I shouldn't stray off-course of established psychology doctrine and protocol. (I eventually hired another editor who was more encouraging.)

The lack of support was very troubling. So, as I continued my search for help to publish this book, a priority concern was finding a publisher willing to provide up-front feedback, based on my stated writing intentions, prior to my making a commitment. Only one publishing company representative consented to this requirement. The feedback he provided proved to be most helpful. He admitted having difficulty seeing how the instructional discussion and the stories, intended to substantiate admittedly uncommon views and advice, were connected. But as we talked about this, eventually he stated, "Okay! Now I get it!" Then, as I asked, he offered suggestions for making it easier for readers to recognize this connection. (This publishing company is AuthorHouse. The representative referred to is Buddy Dow.)

I was still tormented by the felt need for support from family, friends, and colleagues—those who know and love me well, who have firsthand long-term awareness of my deep heartfelt commitment to helping folks not resort to senseless hurtful attempts at well-being. More than a year went by before, with agonizing reluctance, I realized I had to let go this expectation, and returned to AuthorHouse for needed assistance.

After considerable up-front exchange with my trusted AuthorHouse consultant, I felt ready to sign up, and we made a contract that felt right. But then, within days, I was stricken with a fear far more disabling than even the worst demons described in some of my book's stories. I knew I must take seriously the powerful hold of this fear.

A careful review of my life needs and efforts confirmed that I was handling all responsibilities as well as any of us can—that the only possible "too high-risk" involvement had to be signing up with AuthorHouse to publish my book. I was grasping for reasons to cancel our contract, although I wasn't yet ready to admit this cancellation meant I'd actually be deciding to not publish my book at all.

Somehow, once again, my AuthorHouse consultant was brave and caring enough to risk giving the feedback I needed—to not let me give up this lifelong mission, or give up on family and friends and colleagues. (I expect he would say, however, "I was just doing my job—sharing with you what I know to be true and important, trusting you to use well that assistance.")

This interaction in fact gives substance to statements throughout this book acknowledging that it came to be out of a sense of "undone life work" rather than from personal need or ambition—as already stated, I too carry the belief that it's just my job to share what I know to be true and important. (And it also occurs to me, more than any other life experience described in this book, that this final story about the need and power of truthfulness and kindness in helping each other handle demon fears may be the most profound of all.)

It took several days for me to face head-on what the terrible fear was really all about—as I kept revisiting what seemed to be the culprit handicap. I eventually had to admit that I simply couldn't "put myself in the shoes of" persons who didn't feel so honored by my offer to share life lessons learned that they'd grab this gift outright with eager heart and mind. (I know this would be my immediate response to any and all such offers.)

I realized this experience of lack of interest warned that, quite possibly, no one will have interest in the important things I've learned and feel such strong need to share. I thought this might explain the disabling fear referred to. But then a powerful dream took me back through cruel mistreatments suffered, described in some of this book's stories. This dream also brought back upfront awareness that all those hateful "punishments" were provoked by my insistent efforts to enlist remedial attention to serious life threats and responsibilities. So in a sense, in publishing this book, I'm opening the door to further horrible mistreatment. (Yet I'm taking that risk, as I realize that not doing what I know is "the right thing to do" would be even more disabling.)

# *About the Author*

Mary Lax RN, BS, MA
Single mom of five daughters and three sons
(Retired) psychiatric nurse-therapist
Psychologist
Homesteader
Fine-art repro artist
Cello student

I live and work in far north scenic Minnesota with my dog buddy, Akio. My major feat this past year, other than publishing this book, was surviving the worst winter ever—when all that could possibly go wrong did. I've concluded my backwoods lifestyle was easier and safer when I lived even farther up north in a bare-bones primitive house I built myself. But, possibly, that's because I was younger then and better equipped physically to handle brutal conditions. (I do intend to install a woodstove in my current modern well-built house, however, before next winter.)

# *About the Book*

Writing this book is my way of sharing what I've learned in the course of my life on earth—some very unique life experiences and some most of us have in common. I believe it's this information that ought to be shared more freely by all of us, to enable the creation of better ways than wars and prejudices to take care of personal and collective interests and responsibilities.

It's not possible to make life improvements unless we fully own what is and isn't working well. It's also not possible to obtain and provide needed help unless we share what assistance is lacking and available. As a favorite professor insisted at the start of every class, "Our sickness is revealed in our secrets—we must uncover and study what we keep so well hidden before it's possible to cure it."

There are two rules essential to assuring this sharing is productive and non-hurtful. Those key rules are *truthfulness* and *kindness*. The stories in this book represent what happens when these rules are well applied and when they aren't, to encourage careful management of all interactions so that all participants are treated with due respect. There are chapters, as well, that encourage better understanding and use of human emotions and behavior generally.

Made in the USA
San Bernardino, CA
12 June 2019